What About Men?

Dedication

To my two dogs.

ALI PASHA

SOULIMAN THE
MAGNIFICENT

What About Men ?

The Dark and Light Side of the Male

Luc DeSchepper
M.D., Ph.D., Lic.Ac., C.Hom., D.I.Hom.

PUBLISHNG

500 N. Guadalupe St., G441
Santa Fe, NM 87501

ALSO AVAILABLE FROM FULL OF LIFE PUBLISHING

Candida – The Symptoms, The Causes, The Cure

Full of Life – How to achieve and mantain peak immunity

How to Dine Like the Devil and Feel Like a Saint: Good-bye to
   Guilty Eating

Human Condition CRITICAL

Musculoskeletal Diseases and Homeopathy

Acupuncture in Practice

FIRST FULL OF LIFE EDITION PUBLISHED 1995

Library of Congress Catalog Number: 90-090156

ISBN 0-942501-04-7

Acknowledgments

I want to thank my wonderful wife Yolanda for reading the manuscript and giving me insightful advice. It was a pleasure to work with John and Regina of *Word Graphix* in Santa Fe, New Mexico, who made sure this book looks as nice as it does. The real heroes are the innumbrable amount of men and women who have confided in me over all these years, who have divulged their deepest pains and who made me a better doctor.

Luc DeSchepper

M.D., Ph.D., Lic. Ac., C.Hom., D.I.Hom

Contents

Acknowledgments

Introduction ··· 1

ONE
The Five Constitutions and their Relationship ······· **11**
    FIRE – EARTH – METAL – WATER – WOOD ············ 12
    The Generation Cycle ································· 13
    The Control Cycle ······································ 14
    The Destruction Cycle ······························ 15
    Compatibility in Relationships ················· 16
    Recognizing Your Prototype or Constitution: How to
    Read The Next Chapters ···························· 21

TWO
Know Who You Are: A Simple Test ····················· **25**
    Only One Answer Per Question Is Allowed. ········· 25
    Questionnaire ·· 26
    Answer Sheet ··· 29
    Evaluation Sheet. ····································· 30
    Results Recap: ··· 31

THREE
The Wood-Liver Man ···································· **33**
    The Child: A General Already! ····················· 33
    The Adolescent: The Puberty Nightmare ········· 38
    The Adult: A "True" Man ··························· 43
        The Ambitious, Overworked Executive ········· 43
        The Man Who Forgot To Stand Up For Himself ···· 48
        The Oversexed "Wood-Man" ···················· 50

The Ragged Philosopher ···························· 53
The "Wood-Man" ···························· **56**
The Physical Give-Aways And Clues Of The "Wood-
Man" ···························· 58
The "Wood-Man" and His Diseases ···························· 61
How Did He Become a "Wood-Man?" ···························· 62
Causality of the "Wood-Man" ···························· **66**
Supplements and Homeopathic Remedies to Balance
the "Wood-Man" ···························· 66

FOUR

The Fire-Heart Man ···························· **71**
The Child : A Charming Actor ···························· 71
The Teenager: Confused and Humorist ···························· 74
The Heart-Man: the Sensitive Soul ···························· 78
The Universal Reactor ···························· 78
The Talkative, Jealous "Heart-Man" ···························· 82
The Wonderful Performer ···························· 84
The Butterfly Lover ···························· 88
The "Fire-Man" ···························· **91**
The Physical Clues of the "Fire-Man" ···························· 93
The "Fire-Man" and His Diseases ···························· 95
What Made Him a "Fire Man?" ···························· 97
The Impoverished "Fire-Man" ···························· 98
The Happiest Man in the World ···························· 101
The Heartbroken Youth ···························· 103
Causality "Fire-Man" ···························· **108**
Supplements and Homeopathic Remedies to Balance
the "Fire-Man" ···························· 108

FIVE

The Earth-Spleen Man ···························· **111**
The Child: Delayed and Obstinate ···························· 111

The Teenager: Complacent With No Self-confidence 116
The Adult: Good-Natured, Sensitive and Family
  Oriented ·············· 119
  Living in His Own World ·············· 119
  My Digestion Kills Me! ·············· 124
  My Mind Wants, But My Body Can't ·············· 129
The Earth-Man ·············· **131**
The Physical Make-Up of the "Earth-Man" ·············· 132
The "Earth-Man" and His Diseases ·············· 134
How Did He Become an "Earth-Man?" ·············· 135
  The Rock of Gibraltar Crumbles Down ·············· 136
  The Homesick "Earth-Boy" ·············· 140
Causality of the "Earth-Man" ·············· **144**
Supplements and Homeopathic Remedies to Balance
  the "Earth-Man" ·············· 144

Six
The Metal-Lung Man ·············· **147**
  The Child: Frail and Restless ·············· 147
  The Adolescent: Insecure, Withdrawn, and Hungry for
    new Stimuli ·············· 150
  The Adult: the Personification of Atlas, Carrying the
    Globe on His Shoulders ·············· 155
    The Dutiful, Conscientious Family Man ·············· 155
    The Pessimistic and Anxious Hypochondriac ·············· 160
    The Loyal and Frustrated Lover ·············· 163
The "Metal-Man" ·············· **165**
The Physical Clues of the "Metal-Man" ·············· 166
The "Metal-Man" and His Diseases ·············· 168
How Did He Become a "Metal-Man?" ·············· 170
  The "What If" "Lung-Man" ·············· 170
  The Overstressed, Grieving Teenager ·············· 172
Causality of the "Metal-Man" ·············· **176**

Supplements and Homeopathic Remedies for the
"Metal-Man" ·· 176

SEVEN
The Water-Kidney Man ·· **179**
The Child: Introvert, Serious and Fastidious ··········· 179
The Teenager: Tormented and Isolated ···················· 183
The Adult: The Reformer and Perfectionist ············· 187
The Man Who Couldn't Stop Cleaning ················· 187
The Man Who Wanted to Die Since He Was Three
Years-Old ·· 192
The Mind Wants, the Body Refuses ····················· 196
The "Water-Man" ·· **201**
The Physical Characteristics of the "Water-Man" ···· 204
The "Water-Man" and His Diseases ······················· 206
How Did He Become a "Water-Man?" ····················· 208
Abandoned as a Child, Fatigued as an Adult ······· 209
The Man Who Lost His Money and His Health ···· 214
The Man Who Lost His Voice ····························· 218
Causality "Water-Man" ································· **219**
Homeopathic Remedies and Supplements of the
"Water-Man" ·· 220

EIGHT
Violence and Criminality in Men ······························ **223**
Statistics ·· 223
The Five Prototypes and Violence ·························· 224
The "Liver-Wood" Man ································· 224
The "Fire-Heart" Man ································· 228
The "Earth-Spleen" Man ································· 230
The "Metal-Lung" Man ································· 231
The "Water-Kidney" Man ································· 232
The Boy-Killer: a True Story ····························· 234

The O.J. Simpson Trial: Cast of Players ···················· 236
  The Defendant: O.J. ···································· 236
  The Victims: Nicole Brown Simpson and Ronald
    Goldman ·· 238
  The Judge and Attorneys ···························· 240
  Choosing a Jury: For the Prosecution
    and the Defense ···································· 241

Full of Life Publishing: Order Forms

Introduction

I can't leave him now. He needs me more
than ever. The only way I can show him my
love is to take care of him.

When Joan, 42 years-old, first came to see me she was
suffering from scleroderma. She looked haggard and tense
with a mask-like face so typical for this auto-immune disorder, and complaining of all its symptoms. She was over fatigued, had joint stiffness with muscle weakness, and suffered from heartburn and pressure on the esophagus due to
the progressive nature of her disease. Her skin was dry and
hard, she was craving sweets and pastries, and woke up
every morning with a hangover feeling. As a Realtor she
suffered from performance anxiety and had memory blocks
during exams and public speaking. When she had married
Paul 17 years ago, she was a very ambitious woman, outgoing, radiant, slender and graceful with arresting, sparkling
eyes, plenty of self-confidence and dressed in the latest fash-
ions. Yet, when I first saw her, her eyes looked dull and her
limp handshake reflected a lack of self esteem and confidence.

The decline of Joan's health appears to have started four
years ago when a series of family mishaps occurred. Looking for the triggering factor of her disease, Joan was not going to shift responsibility to some one else.

Really, my husband is wonderful. He is
introspective, can be very charming, and is
very intelligent. He never forgets my
birthday and goes to the children's soccer

1

games. I guess I am not able to do enough
for the family.

She told me that Paul was very successful in everything
he wanted to do, and in spite of a busy schedule, used to
have always time for his children.

I guess, everyone in the neighborhood
envied us. Paul is very good-looking,
always showed great respect for me and
has a romantic nature. He would bring
flowers home for no special reason and
surprised me with idyllic dinners out. He
was the man made in heaven.

As I listened to Joan, it was hard for me to imagine why
someone in such happy circumstances would look as pallid
as she did. Obviously, she did not tell me everything. As a
physician trained in alternative medicines, I am always looking for the cause and effect of each illness. So far, nothing in
Joan's story would explain to me this auto-immune condition that seemed to have come on like a vengeance and destroyed not only her outer beauty but her soul as well. There
was a complete contradiction in what I heard and what I
saw. What changed such a successful career women, a go-
getter, into a fearful, low self-confident person?

I pressed her gently to tell me some more about the year
that "was the worst one in her life." It had clearly been the
turning point not only for her, but for the whole family as
well.

My husband never thought it could happen
to him. He always succeeded in everything

he wanted to do, and money was always
plentiful. But that year he had put everything on the wrong horse. The business
failed, and we had to sell our house. I could
have lived with all this were it not for my
husband's behavior. I always perceived
him as the Rock of Gibraltar, self-confident,
cocky and witty. But from the first crisis
moment, he fell apart and suffered a tremendous nervous breakdown.

Joan began to cry as she continued talking about what
she recalled as her most heartbreaking days. It had nothing
to do with the material loss but much more with the ruin of
the perceived image she had of her husband.

I never thought he could fall so low as to
attempt suicide. I became the sole caretaker
of my husband, the failed business and the
rest of the family. To make matters worse,
some unresolved conflicts between my
eldest son and my husband came to a head.
I was constantly pulled between these two
forces and any choice between the two
would have been devastating to me. As it
was, I could not prevent my son from
leaving home that same year. I was devastated. I guess I failed as a mother because I
couldn't keep the family together. I have
never been the same since.

As I listened to Joan, somehow her story hit home. Her
plight was so similar to many others I had heard in my 25

year career as a physician. There was no doubt in my mind that the traumas four years ago were the onset for the heavy price Joan was paying now. How could this have been prevented? It would be too easy to put the blame on Paul. But one thing was certain. Paul did not behave like the husband she thought she married and Joan was ultimately overwhelmed by the grief, the guilt and the monumental responsibility that befell her. Her Rock of Gibraltar failed, and the emotional stress of that failure, by far, surpassed all the material losses she suffered. What a price to pay! I thought, what if Joan and every woman in this world, would have a guideline to choose a partner, something as close as possible to a scientific approach, with objective as well as subjective guidelines. What if Joan could read a book which explained how to look at physical and emotional signals in a man, that would provide more insight than just counting on instinct, intuition and love at first sight, to help her choose her partner for life?

Of course, any relationship should grow slowly so that one can see the partner in different circumstances, not just on a date or in a social setting. But that common sense usually goes out the door when two people are overpowered by infatuation. Who doesn't like romance? Alas. All too often romantic blinders keep the relationship in the dark and it is rare indeed that this romance lasts forever. Because often, it was based purely on fantasy. She will say things such as, "He could not stop phoning me," "He would skip a meal just to be with me," "He would bring flowers just to show how much he loved me." And he always told me "I never met anyone like you before." This does not necessarily mean deceptiveness on the man's part. We all remember whirlwind courtships that swept us off our feet. Little mistakes in the partner are "cute," and his outgoing personality and heavy socializing makes you think how lucky you are that he wants to be with you.

If he is that popular and he makes you feel that wanted, he *must* be the greatest! When he lies, you think he is doing it to save your feelings. Yet, years later, repetitive mistakes become a nuisance, his socializing and partying isolates you more and more at home, and frankly, you find out that his lies are a way to justify the childish behavior he has always shown.

Acupuncture and homeopathy are truly ancient sciences. What makes a science is not the collection of facts, but the organization and formulation of those facts in principles and laws. Both of these sciences have been the result of years and years of observation, confirmed for hundred of years thereafter by clinical work. It might come as a shock to you, but one needs only to closely study the history of modern medicine to discover that most of its findings are really accidental, and not the result of pure scientific thinking. If humans want to predict with more certainty, I would say, with almost scientific certainty, who their partners should be, then we will have to rely on sciences that take the whole person in account: mental, emotional and physical. This has always been the pillar on which alternative medicines survived and was never matched, even now, by Western medicine. Therefore it occurred to me, that using acupuncture and homeopathy in describing the constitution, or the sum of all the characteristics in a person, is as close to science as we can come in selecting a suitable partner.

As young people, we all have a dream picture of our future partner. We often have a set description as what this partner should look like, how he should behave and how he will bring us happiness forever! Why then is there a 50% divorce rate in most States? Because, like modern medicine, our selection is mostly based on a hit-and-miss situation. How often have I heard my female patients telling me: "I wish there was something I could have looked out for when I met him first, some tell tale signs but I just followed my heart." There is nothing wrong in listening to your heart, but this book wants to give you physical, emotional and mental signs you can actually see in the person in front of you. "Does he match your dream picture now?" Sure, some people are very good at deceit but I have yet to see the first person who is able to fake his total physical and psychological picture. Do you know why? Because that person might know how to use some deceit and flattery but he does not know the physical signs that will expose his constitution, unless he studied acupuncture and homeopathy or unless he reads this book that describes the whole person, not just his physical being, not just his mental and emotional picture.

A lot of self-help books for women I have read are written by psychotherapists. For the most part, the goal of these books is to teach women to stand up for themselves, take charge of their own lives and ban the classical man-monster out of their life. That is like trying to repair the situation after the damage is done. What is wrong with this picture too, is that very often it reflects the painful situation the psychotherapist has once experienced herself. I had enough psychotherapists as patients in my office who behaved very aggressively to show me how far beyond their previous heartbreak they were, how by "dwelling over the past", they felt now much better and were taking charge of their lives. They would be very good therapists indeed, for people in the *same* situation. But trying to group together all people who went through the same trauma and applying the same technique, is committing the same cardinal sin as Western medicine that groups patients in catalogues of disease pictures and then looks for a common therapy. Not everyone reacts to the same trauma in the same way. Some people might react to grief with complete isolation and not show as much as one tear (silent grief) while others might overflow their friends with cascades of tears. In effect, the particular emotional manner of reacting to the impact of mental, emotional and physical factors, constitutes for each individual the most finished and exact expression of *his or her* temperament which he brought into this world. There is no wrong or right here, just different people. This is why I don't believe that all women want to be Gloria Steinem. Some want a husband who provides for them and are pleased with an uneventful life at home, their castle. Others want adventure and excitement and continuous changes. Joan wanted to have an equally strong partner, not one who fell apart at the first sight of trouble. Some women find their happiness in making their house spotlessly clean: remodeling and refurnishing is their true merriment. And yes, some want to be out there in the world, making decisions and want no part of being tied to home by children. Should we condemn some of them? Of course not! What is more important and what this book wants to answer, is to give to each of these women the opportunity to meet the men who will respect their choice of life. Not men who will try to change them later in the marriage, but men who are compatible with *the women's* dreams, and not with the picture the psychotherapist or husband have in mind.

Before you can change any relationship, and even better, before you enter one, you have to be able to *do* something different. Too many people blindly enter an alliance with a man and hope for the best as they go along. Hoping and praying is one thing, but clearly observing objective and subjective signs in a man and understanding what they mean, puts any woman in a winning position.

To help you accomplish this, I have described five different prototypes of men based on acupuncture and homeopathic observations. I will describe the men with their good and bad qualities and the interaction they have with women in their lives. This book will let you know if the man in your life will have a tendency to control you, stimulate you or be chaotic for you. I let the men speak for themselves as they came to me with their hopes and questions. This is not a book only for women. Men will read about their flaws, the kinks in their armor and therefore be able to correct them with supplements and homeopathic remedies *before* they are translated into the diseases, which I will predict will occur with a certainty, for each of these types. There is no doubt that an association between any kind of woman and man can be successful. However, through scientific homeopathic and acupuncture laws, I will be able to predict great relationships, not-so-great ones and real catastrophic situations as I will show what types should never marry each other unless they are able to weather the hurricanes that will come their way through diligent work and communication.

Along the way, I will introduce to you some patients I treated in my practice. All names and identifying characteristics have of course been changed to preserve their privacy. But the situations described are real. Women readers will recognize the men—husband, child(ren), boss, friend—in their lives. They will never look at them the same way again but with a different degree of understanding making them less vulnerable, and more effective in their choice of partner. And if you are married/involved with a prototype with whom you aren't suitable, you *can* change him. With the help of a homeopathic physician, a constitutional remedy which I will describe for each type, and inexpensive supplements can change the personality of a human being. We should not cling to the idea that the constitution is something static and motionless, but rather be aware that it is *dynamic* and *functional*. Therapy can be economical, fast and gentle. How often I have heard in my practice, "I can't believe the change in that man since you treated him. I always thought he was a rough diamond, but now he is polished and a joy to be around."

As you read about these different men, you will smile as you recognize some people in your life, or you might cry as you see the type you were linked to in a failed partnership. But now it will make sense to you. You will throw off your guilt and, with a smile and new weapons, look forward with confidence to meeting just the right one for *you*. You will have my love and understanding every step of the way.

ONE

The Five Constitutions and their Relationship

Western medicine still views illness as a misplacement or wear and tear of spare parts. Healing, therefore, in their books is simply replacement or mending those bad parts. Chinese Traditional Medicine, established 5,000 years ago is, on the other hand, an energetic medicine. It is not the only one. Homeopathy, brought to humankind by Samuel Hahnemann (°1755-†1843), stresses the overall importance of the strength of "Qi or Vital Energy." What makes them essentially different from modern medicine is that these alternative medicines have been able to organize their observations in the formulation of laws and principles. For the intelligent practice of Western medicine, simplification is necessary. Phenomena which at present are so difficult to understand due to their diversity are all produced in few simple ways. What is now so complicated and difficult will become simplified and easy to understand once allopathic medicine follows the roads of holistic medicines.

The concept of Yin and Yang are two terms found in any explanation of Chinese medicine. This principle allows one to classify all the observations in two entities, one Yin, the other Yang. When we mention Yin or Yang, that only means *preponderant* Yin or Yang: there is neither absolute Yin or Yang. While they are each other's opposites, they are each other's complement; the one cannot exist without the other.

They are both necessary. While the Yin usually refers to women and Yang to men, we find also Yin referring to the dark side in men, and Yang to the light side in women. Another classification system is found in the *Five Elements and its Laws*. The Chinese again were able to classify all observations into these five elements. These elements interact through cycles of activation and inhibition. What are these elements?

FIRE – EARTH – METAL – WATER – WOOD

These five elements are five totalities with five organs and five hollow organs (Figure 1). They correspond to our five prototypes of men.

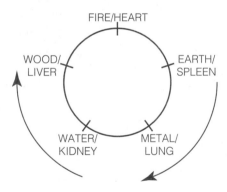

Figure 1

Normally the Earth element would be placed in the center, but for reasoning purposes, it is put on the circle. Several important laws will dominate these five elements: the *Generation cycle, the Controlling cycle* and *the Destruction cycle.*

The Generation Cycle

These five elements are by no means inert or immovable. In the Generation cycle, a certain element (or prototype) activates another one, which in turn, activates the next one. This always goes clockwise (Figure 1).

- Fire activates the Earth.
- Earth activates Metal.
- Metal activates Water.
- Water activates Wood.
- Wood activates Fire.

It needs to be well understood that each organ does not provide energy to the next organ in the cycle, just like one prototype of men will not give energy to the next person (female or male) in the cycle. Rather, it activates or *stimulates* the organ or the person that follows in the Generation cycle This gives us the following law:

"Each organ (person) activates the element (person) that follows and is activated by the organ (person) that precedes it."

All this may not be clear at first, but a few examples will clarify this frequently-used concept in acupuncture.

- Fire activates or produces Earth: the Fire burns everything to ashes, which will be mixed with the Earth.
- Earth produces Metal: the metals are found in the earth and are produced there.
- Metal produces Water: any metal at a certain temperature becomes liquid.
- Water produces Wood: any wood or

vegetation needs water for its growth.

· Wood produces Fire: the first fire was made with the help of wood.

The Control Cycle

To keep an equilibrium in this world, there is no production without control. (Figure 3)

· Water controls the Fire: this is self-evident.

· Wood controls the Earth: wood or vegetation covers the earth; the stronger the vegetation, the less earth is seen.

· Fire controls the Metal: self-evident.

· Earth controls the Water: when it rains, most of the water is absorbed by the earth.

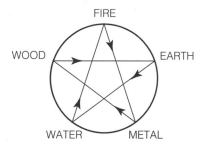

Figure 2

The Destruction Cycle

This is the opposite of the Control cycle: a certain element (person) becomes so strong that it (s/he) reverses the more natural Control cycle. (Figure 3)

Figure 3

How do we know that an element or person is strong or weak? This will become clear to the reader once the different constitutions are described. To be complete, outlined in Table 1 are all the characteristics of the Five elements. Later it will help to determine the weak and strong points of the different prototypes.

Table 1 Characteristics of the Five Elements

Wood	Fire	Earth	Metal	Water
Spring	Summer	5th Season	Fall	Winter
Fong	Heat	Dampness	Dryness	Cold
Acidity	Bitter	Sweet	Pungent	Salty
West	South	Center	East	North
Blood	Psyche	Flesh	Energy	Will
Nails	Face Color	Lips	Hair-Body	Hair
Eyes	Tongue	Mouth	Nose	Ear
Eye Sight	Taste	Touch	Smell	Hearing
Tears	Sweat	Saliva	Mucus	Urine
Anger	Happiness	Worry	Sadness	Fear
Walking	Observing	Sitting	Lying	Standing
Sheep	Chicken	Beef	Horse	Pork
Green	Red	Yellow	Blue	Black
Speaking	Salivation	Swallowing	Coughing	Yawning

Compatibility in Relationships

Looking at these Nature Laws, we can predict what marriages will be made in heaven (or have at least a greater chance to succeed) and which ones will be made in hell. It should be clear that we are not talking only about marriages. We are talking about relationships with friends, a boss, children, parents, parents-in-law, etc. Recognizing in further chapters to what prototype they belong and to which one you belong, will make it clear why you have a good or bad connection with them.

Two people belonging to the same element, WOOD-WOOD for instance, *have an excellent chance to survive any difficulties.* Belonging to the same element means that they have quite a bit in common. They will have the same physical stamina and physical built, an identical physical or sex drive and, emotionally/mentally, they will often react in the same manner. For instance, the "Wood" type will erupt very easily with anger, but just like a volcano, will as quickly calm down. Both partners understand this phenomenon and will have an easy time adjusting to it. They are almost like twins who feel and know in advance how their partner will react and why he is doing it that way. Their ambitions and interests are the same. They will both like to travel and be adventurous, rather than to sit at home like the "Earth" type. It is almost uncanny, but understandable, that they both will like similar music, sports, food and sex. With so much in common, don't you think that the odds for a good marriage are on their side? Even when one of the partners is "stronger" than the other one, they still will stimulate each other rather than feel controlled and threatened by the other spouse. She won't have to "walk on eggs" or withdraw in suppressed anger so as to not set him off. Neither does he bewilder you by switching behavior from charm to rage within seconds. She knows the storm will blow over as quickly as it started. Being herself a "Liver" or "Wood" type, she understands that she is better off by letting him free some steam by himself, rather than criticizing him or even soothing him with words. He will have none of this. Once this hurricane is over, he will not hold a grudge and easily forgets the incident. Of course, when he is the type who becomes more unbalanced with more storms in his life than balmy periods, it is time to stabilize him through the matching homeopathic remedy and supplements. This will become clear later in the book. So, if you find that you and your partner belong to the same element in the Generation cycle—Fire-Fire, Earth-Earth, etc.—you have all the ingredients for a long-lasting, happy alliance. It is like finding your long-lost soul mate who gives you equality in the relationship, asks for your opinion and feelings, values your achievements and takes part of the blame if anything goes wrong. You are allowed to have your own interests and friends without making him unhappy and jealous.

There is another group of people who have an almost identical chance at succeeding in marriage and friendship than the previous one: *two elements (persons) which succeed each other in the Generation cycle.* For instance, a "Wood-Liver" man and a "Fire-Heart" woman. As you can see in Figure 1, they follow each other clockwise in the Generation or Production cycle. Rather than having many characteristics in common, these two types will *stimulate or feed* each other.

Like a natural flow, the "Wood-Man" will allow growth and free expression of the "Fire-Woman." In fact, this man is capable of bringing out the best in his female partner as their Energy flows easily together in a harmonious, unobstructive way. The "Wood-Man" will guess intuitively what direction his "Fire-Woman" is going to take and use his talents and energy to help her achieve her goal in an almost effortless, invisible way. At the same token, the "Heart-Woman" will not deplete the "Wood-Man" of his energy, just like a balanced child will not exhaust a giving, loving mother. Both benefit from the relationship: the receiver because of the intense support felt, the giver because of the rewards and love and appreciation. This is the kind of relationship that will turn heads; there is a tireless interaction between both partners. Like a connecting pipe line they constantly exchange love, attention, interests and respect in a playful manner. Of course, the above is also true for a "Wood-Woman" and a "Fire-Man" relationship. You can predict for yourself, looking at Figure 1, what other relationships have a high degree of success: Fire-Earth, Earth-Metal, Metal-Water and Water-Wood.

One step below the two previous marriages *are the ones formed in the Control cycle* (see Figure 2). As the name implies, it is obvious that one of the partners will be much stronger than the other one. While this may not be a good solution to the "Gloria Steinem" female, this relationship is not automatically doomed to failure. Take for instance a "Wood-Man" and an "Earth-Woman." There is no doubt that the "Wood-Man" will be the breadwinner of the family. He will make the most important decisions of their life: how to spend the money, education for the children, vacations to take, and even the kind of food that will come in the house. No doubt the father in this household will be the dominant figure, but not necessarily to the detriment of the other partner. An "Earth-Woman" is very pleased with an uneventful life spent at home. The love for the home, their "castle," means everything to her. She dislikes the pressure from the outside and therefore easily relinquishes the responsibilities of making a living in a competitive world to her husband who thrives on tug-of-war situations. She will not resent the "general's" role of her husband, but makes an ideal "soldier" admiring the jest and courage of her commander. Don't feel sorry for this woman. She is the rock at home, the down-to-earth woman, who is the chief-of-staff often surprising her husband with solutions he never thought of. Just like in the army, communication between these two parties, will be cordial, respectful and beneficial to the whole household. More than ever, this woman is the one in the expression "Behind every successful man, is a strong woman." Of course there is a slight danger. Commonly, a "Wood-Man" gets caught up in the competitive stressful world around him. If the forgets to listen to the mothering, wise "Earth-Woman" he can forget the most common life-style rules. He starts smoking, eats junk foods, drinks large amounts of coffee to perform and often, takes drugs to enhance his performance. The balance between this man and his "Earth-Spouse" can be broken: the burnt-out "Wood-Man" neglects the useful hints of his closest adviser and becomes overbearing, unresponsive and withdrawn. At this point, the constitutional homeopathic remedy can achieve miracles. It is obvious that relationships in the Control cycle are in a more delicate balance than the ones in the Generation cycle. It is easier in this cycle to be out of balance: the "Wood-Man" yells easily, gets irritated by any of his mate's suggestions, blames her for everything that goes wrong in and outside of the relationship and reduces the stubborn, strong "Earth-Woman" to a fearful creature, with a lack of self-esteem and low self-confidence. Apparently, the relationship needs some fast mending before it is irreparably damaged. The same can be said of other relationships in the Control cycle: Earth-Water, Water-Fire, Fire-Metal and Metal-Wood. Any of these associations will thrive on a more delicate balance and often need more work than the ones in the Generation cycle.

And last but not least, we come to the marriages made in hell. They are the *ones caught in the Destruction cycle* (Figure 3). We see in Figure 3 that this Destruction cycle is the opposite of the Control cycle: elements that are supposed to be in a more dominated position become "excessive," predominant and controlling, opposite to Nature's Laws. Because it is not a situation common in nature unless one partner becomes too weak, the relationship becomes uncomfortable and unbearable for the suppressed party. Take for instance, an "Earth-Mother" dominating the "Wood-Man." The otherwise "wise" woman and down-to-earth adviser becomes a nagging woman, clipping the wings of her "Wood-Man" who feels stuffed, overwhelmed and oppressed. The "Earth-Woman" becomes an obsessive compulsive manipulator who pays more attention to the neatness of her house than the more pressing issues in life like encouragement, love, respect, and leaving space for the spouse. She nags him continually about his habits of not eating neatly, not dressing sharply, not folding his cloths as she wants him to, not putting his shoes on the right space, not putting the toilet seat down, etc. This will have two consequences to the "Wood-Man:" either he will become a miserable, depressed, lazy philosopher, quite a turn from the brilliant entrepreneur he once was; or he will bring all his strength together in a negative way and erupt with a burst of frustrated anger, often leading to violence. The problem in this "Destructive cycle" relationship is that we deal with both spouses in imbalance. Very often neither one of the parties wants to give an inch and recurrent explosive situations are a result of it.

A classical example of this relationship "made in hell" is seen in the movie "Fatal Attraction." She is an extreme "Fire-Heart" possessive human being, only living for passion and danger. He is the indecisive, more anxious "Water-Kidney" type, insecure about his marriage at home and overpowered and seduced by the loquacity and snake-like seductiveness of her. The result is catastrophical. The snake does not let go of her prey until the "Water-Man" becomes decisive enough to escape this strangling situation and kills her, the ultimate form of restoring Nature's control cycle as it was established (Figure 2). Other cancerous combinations can be the Wood controlling the Metal, the Water controlling the Earth and the Metal controlling the Fire (see Figure 3).

Recognizing Your Prototype or Constitution: How to Read The Next Chapters

In the next chapters, the five different constitutions will be analyzed with a description from childhood on. It is very important to realize that your *real* constitution will be recognized in your first five years of existence. As we evolve further in life, many events, physical and emotional, will add *layers* on top our beginning constitutional layer. Therefore, in psychotherapy as well as in homeopathy, a cure is established by peeling those layers off like you would peel an onion: you start with the last layer working your way back to the original, constitutional layer. Therefore it is not uncommon that you would say after reading this book, "I recognize I am a "Wood" type now, but I used to be an "Earth" type." Most likely your constitution was "Earth" but you changed into a "Wood" type later because of a certain event. One of those would be an indignation situation: a continuous verbal, physical or emotional abusive situation, would change the passive, withdrawn "Earth" type in a more irritable, angry "Wood" type. More about triggering factors, which will add different layers above your constitution, will be discussed in later chapters.

It is sufficient that you see a majority of the characteristics of one type matching your personality to know that you are in that type *at that moment*. For instance, if 50% of what you read about a "Wood" type relates to you, then that is what you are. Don't say: "I don't have this and that of what you describe in a "Wood" type, so I can't be a "Wood-Man" or "Wood-Woman." What you are doing then is called *negative* matching. Not ONE person on earth has *all* the characteristics of a "Wood-Person." He might have 90% of the characteristics, and even more, but *never* 100%! Remember, there is always Yin in Yang and vice versa. When you try to find out what your constitution is, or your husband's, child's, friend's, etc, you do *positive* matching. Yes, he has this and that trait according to what you outlined in the "Wood" type. In fact, the majority of what you summarize in the "Wood" matches him.

Now that you know what you are looking for, I wish you an exciting journey in understanding and analyzing the relationships you have with the most important people in your life. And remember, if you already know that the relationship is not doing well, solutions to improve it are offered. For those lucky souls basking in a healthy happy relationship, you can strengthen your emotional and physical health even more by applying the constitutional homeopathic remedy. Everyone around you, and above all *you* , will benefit from it!

TWO

Know Who You Are:
A Simple Test

Knowing yourself and the man in your life is not such an easy task as you might imagine. The purpose of this book is to make this possible. By responding to the following questions, and adding a score at the end, you will be able to determine to which of the five prototypes yourself and the man in your life belongs. This will enable you to focus on the chapter for each specific type and guide you in understanding and helping the man in your life. Knowing your and your partner's constitution will enable you to determine the nature of your relationship according to the laws explained in Chapter One.

Answer the questions and enter the score on the answer sheet, which follows the questionnaire. Use the following scale:

Very · · · · · · if the total of what is said responds completely to you: score 10

Sufficient · if a part of the expression does not correspond to you, but the rest fits you very well: score 5

Little · · · · · if one or more of the expression does not fit you and the rest very little: score 2

Not · · · · · · · if none of what is said corresponds to you: score 0

Only One Answer Per Question Is Allowed.

Questionnaire

1. Frustrated by lack of improvement in government issues and political behavior.

2. You consider yourself to be envied and jealous at the same time.

3. You are introverted, quiet, shy and amiable.

4. Easily discouraged, depressed and anxious for the future.

5. Good listener to other people's problems but a very private person reluctant to express your inner feelings.

6. Love for order, discipline and law.

7. Indecisive, changeable, hesitant self-pity.

8. Gets burned out because of trying to undertake too much and too fast.

9. Likes pleasantries and jokes, word games and puzzles.

10. Easily withdrawn by yourself, writes a private diary.

11. A go-getter, hard working, fast-living.

12. Likes poetry and novels.

13. Likes to hug, touch and kiss.

14. Good self-discipline, pride, directness and selfish.

15. Vulnerable, sensitive but quick-minded and charming.

16. Very fearful and anxious: to be alone, of health, claustrophobia, etc. You are a natural "worry-wart."

17. Always wants to be the center of attention: at family gatherings, parties, discussions and lectures.

18. Will not start arguing but rather withdraws and protests with stubbornness.

19. Always too over prepared for any task, sense of perfectionism is important.

20. Does not like to be physical: not too much exercise, tries to reduce physical activity to a minimum.

21. Critical, intolerant and impatient with people who are late, do sloppy work, and prepare poorly.

22. Loves anything stimulating and exciting in life: food, work, drugs, alcohol, sex, new plans.

23. Wants consolation and hugs in grief or heartbreak.

24. Very meticulous, fastidious and detailed in anything you do, write or say.

25. Pleased with an uneventful life, with the family as the center of attention.

26. Very analytical, let the mind rule over the passion when resolving problems.

27. Everything you say is well-thought in slow words, without passion.

28. Easily irritated by slowness of other people, does not pay attention to detail.

29. Romantic, playful, friendly, engaging, and optimistic.

30. Very dogmatic, methodical and according to the rules; justice is important.

31. Does not take initiative easily, but rather undergoes passively what happens in life.

32. Is very loyal in love, romantic and melancholic.

33. Timid, sentimental, and fragile to the point of depression.

34. Easily dominates the conversation because of his knowledge and his love for studying and reading.

35. Loves the good life: eating, being with friends, going out and sleeping in.

36. Does not like to spend easily, always thinks about the future when saving money.

37. Likes to draw attention to himself using seductive manners, proud attitude and fashionable dressing.

38. Takes command easily, decides and executes quickly.

39. Does not like unexpected things to happen, never will deviate one iota from a plan, prefers to organize life in advance.

40. Your main concern is maintaining your health and avoiding diseases; you have fear of catching a disease and fear of death.

Answer Sheet

Remember, enter the score from to the following rating scale in the blank for each question. Make a copy of this page for each additional person being tested.

Not	Little	Sufficient	Very
0	2	5	10

1. _____   11. _____   21. _____   31. _____

2. _____   12. _____   22. _____   32. _____

3. _____   13. _____   23. _____   33. _____

4. _____   14. _____   24. _____   34. _____

5. _____   15. _____   25. _____   35. _____

6. _____   16. _____   26. _____   36. _____

7. _____   17. _____   27. _____   37. _____

8. _____   18. _____   28. _____   38. _____

9. _____   19. _____   29. _____   39. _____

10. _____   20. _____   30. _____   40. _____

Evaluation Sheet.

After completing all the questions, transfer your scores from the answer sheet to the evaluation sheet below. Be careful filling in the scores, since the questions are no longer in numeric order. Then add up the total score in each column. Make a copy of this page for each additional person being tested.

Wood	Fire	Earth	Metal	Water
1. _2_	2. _0_	3. _2_	4. _0_	7. _2_
8. _0_	9. _10_	5. _2_	6. _2_	10. _0_
11. _5_	12. _6_	13. _5_	26. _5_	14. _2_
17. _2_	15. _10_	18. _2_	27. _5_	16. _0_
22. _2_	23. _10_	20. _10_	30. _5_	19. _2_
28. _5_	29. _10_	25. _5_	32. _5_	21. _5_
34. _5_	33. _0_	31. _5_	36. _10_	24. _5_
38. _10_	37. _0_	35. _10_	39. _2_	40. _0_
Tot. _31_	Tot. _40_	Tot. _41_	Tot. _34_	Tot. _16_

Results Recap:

Wood-Type: _____

Fire-Type: _____

Earth-Type: _____

Metal-Type: _____

Water-Type: _____

The dominant character is the highest score, the second character second highest score and so on.

After answering these 40 questions, you will get a test score that is accurate in more than 80% of the cases. The number one type according to the score (highest score) is the dominant character of the patient, which he manifests most on any given day. Previous statistics have shown that approximately 50% of the persons tested will be defined as belonging to ONE type only. This means that either the person himself, or someone else who knows him, will recognize the tested individual when the statements in the questions are read aloud.

It is also interesting to find out if one's parents fall into the same category as the person tested. In this case it is clear that the patient has inherited all the characteristics from his parents (called miasm in homeopathy). Once you find out to what type you belong, you will recognize yourself in the types described in further chapters. It will provide you with invaluable tools such as how to choose the right partner and how to avoid disease by reinforcing your weak points through supplements and homeopathic remedies.

Some readers will recognize themselves in two or even

three types. For instance your highest score is in the "Wood"type, but "Fire" scores a close second (the dominant type is followed closely by a second type). This of course shows the diversity one can have within one type. You can have a "Wood" type with a lot of passion, restlessness and hurried mind (equals "Fire") versus a "Wood" type with stubbornness, laziness and bad eating habits (equals "Earth"). There is another possibility: you score evenly on two types! For instance the person is equally a "Fire" and "Earth" type: this will explain how a passionate (equals "Fire") human being can be obese (equals "Earth"). A combination of "Wood-Water" is driven to do a lot of things but being Water, he wants to do them perfectly which will stop the natural speed of action of the "Wood" type. All this becomes very clear as you start reading the next chapters. When you read, start by reading the chapter of your highest score type, followed by the second highest score type. Your own personality, or the one of the person you test, will become clear. You will truly know yourself and anyone else!

THREE

The Wood-Liver Man

The Child: A General Already!

> I don't know anymore what to do with
> Andrew. At school, he is lazy and disrup-
> tive. At home, he is messy while he eats. He
> never sits still and is only happy when the
> TV or radio blares out loud noises. He
> drives me crazy and I am exhausted.

Laura had a desperate look on her face while she kept an anxious eye on her 7 year-old son, who was viewing me with a curiosity bordering on defiance. His lively eyes were scanning me hoping I would be a better challenge than his poor mother. Just before coming into my office, Laura had to spank Andrew, because as she moaned with exasperation, "he has to touch everything in the waiting room."Not that it stopped Andrew for long. Next he threw his attention on everyone else and proceeded to organize a game with three other children, telling them exactly what to do. He was yelling orders at them, which to the amazement of the adults, were followed up with a swiftness they did not expect from their children. Was this their child who never listened when ordered to eat slower or to get ready in the morning for school? Who was this little bully who in minutes took charge of their kids and formed them into a subchapter of the Boy Scouts under their very own eyes?

> Look at him, Doctor. Look at his hair flying
> all over the place. And these are his new
> clothes. Look at them: already dirty, his
> shirt hanging out of his pants and he is
> falling over his untied shoes.

If Laura, who was a rather tidy mother, was embarrassed at the behavior and look of her son, it did not show the least in Andrew. He did not seem to care a bit about his appearance but rather carried it as a badge of honor that he stood out in the crowd by being different.

> His teacher tells me he can do a lot better
> than he does now. He just does not seem to
> be a bit interested in most subjects except
> when it comes to history. Then he already
> knows many things and does not hesitate
> to correct the teacher to the amusement of
> his friends. Oh yes. He is very popular
> among his fellow students. He is always
> sought out to direct the game and divide
> them into groups. I guess they like him
> because he allows everyone to participate,
> even the smallest ones.

While his mother was painting a "painful" portrait of Andrew, he already had withdrawn on a chair as to show his ennui with the conversation. He was reading his book. Not to my amazement, it was the *Guinness Book of World Records*. When I asked Andrew about the most impressive feat he read in there, he proceeded to lecture me about five different records, told in such accuracy and detail, that it puzzled Laura, who was thinking to put him in a slower learning class because he seemed to be too "dumb" for his present class.

> It is funny, Doctor. He seems to have this enormous photographic memory but at school, he is sulky, rude to the teacher, continuously distracted by everything that goes on *outside* of the classroom. His teacher thinks he can do so much better with his school work if only he showed some more diligence and care.

Laura did not seem to understand that this typical "Liver" child was actually very intelligent, ahead of everyone else. But everything went too slow for Andrew: he was bored stiff at school. The subjects were not exciting enough and the teacher continuously had to repeat himself for the other children. That's when someone like Andrew "checks out" and dabbles in his own exciting fantasy world. This is where he rehearses the roles of his heroes he read about in his "book of facts." In his daydreams, he breaks the existing long-jump record, amidst the admiring shouts of the spectators. As a Julius Caesar, he is doing his honor round around the stadium until, "Andrew! Stop daydreaming." His teacher just brought him back to the same old routine reality.

> You know, Doctor. The only time Andrew is not slamming doors and tumbling downstairs is when he can watch our neighbor, Joe, tinkering at his lawn mower or motorcycle. He seems to be fascinated by tools

and can stand there for hours watching him.

The "Wood-Liver" boy has but one fear: being bored! That's why he is continuously in motion; sitting still and waiting are pure torture for him. Time always goes too slowly. Being active is a must for him and skate boarding, playing soccer or riding his bike alleviate a lot of the inner tension and mass of energy bottled up in his little body. Have you seen those little boys at the airport strung on a dog's lease to a mother who continuously needs to pull the lease to keep the child from wandering off? It is the curiosity at play of the "Wood-Boy" from young age on. His stature is lanky and wirey, he looks like a whip and behaves like one. He has big eyes, which accentuate the frank look he often shows in his defiance, offset by large eyebrows. His intelligence shows in early recognition of valued objects. He will know the word "antique" before anyone else and becomes a collector at young age. "Liver-Boys" are collectors in every sense. He will put away some hard earned money and will feel the pleasure of just counting it on his bed from time to time, without any urge to spend it. You can imagine it is like pulling teeth when you want to borrow from him and he rarely shares his toys with other boys. "What is his is his" is clearly established and only under his close supervision and under his guidance, can other children play with his toys. Of course, as smart as he is, he is always willing to bargain with his friends. They should be watching out. They should know that this "Wood-Boy" will always come out on top. With his convincing speech, he gives his friends the impression they are getting a great deal, but of course, the only one getting the biggest stick is himself. Even when playing cards, he hates to lose. Collecting victories is as important as having fun at the game. Often, when he loses, he will profess to be bored with the game and abruptly stops playing, leaving his friends at wits end. He will be insensitive to their desire to continue and urges them to do exactly what he wants.

His messiness drives any mother crazy unless she is a "Liver" type herself. Having two "Liver-Boys" myself, I see that they could turn an obsessive compulsive mother (the "Earth" type) into a nervous wreck from morning on. They hate being washed, but after pushing them under the shower, they always proceed to inundate the bathroom. Coming out of the shower, they drop the towels right on the floor in the water while dirty cloths are competing with towels for water absorption. Any wise mother slaps a warning on the door: "Attention! "Wood-Boy" at work. Proceed with caution." Indeed the innocent "Earth-Boy" coming after him will slip all over the towels and wet clothes left behind. He can't find the soap, the shampoo is running in the shower, and the toothpaste cap is left off the tube so that the toothpaste is oozing all over the sink, making "beautiful" designs.

The "Earth-Mother" will continuously struggle with the "Wood-Boy" about not being dressed warmly enough. The chilly "Earth-Mother," projecting her own cold-intolerance, pushes pullovers on him. But for the "Wood-Boy," sweaters are defined as "something he has to wear when his mother is cold." He is warm-blooded and kicks the blankets away at night, leaving his windows open to allow fresh air cool off his body as well as his temperament. His fierce independence will be another source of struggle with his mother. He wants to dress by himself (and that includes not tucking his shirt in his pants), he wants to wipe himself after passing stool, with the result that his underpants are always stained and smelly and he wants to wipe his own nose. Unfortunately, he always seems to miss the biggest boogers, which are drying up next to his nose. There is a constant conflict between the mother trying him to teach the rules of the house and the inability of the child to be subservient. Rather than obeying, he runs away, cries, becomes irritable, and throws a temper tantrum to show the displeasure of losing his well-guarded independence. Harsh words and corporal punishment are no help. These "Wood-Boys" are very resilient tough little creatures who take the punishment in stride without crying too much. In fact they feel more insulted than hurt. You want to smoothen this rough diamond? Give him the constitutional homeopathic remedy: Sulphur.

The Adolescent: The Puberty Nightmare

> Please do something about Paul, Doctor. I
> am afraid that his father is going to kill him
> if he does not change.

That was the unexpected response to my question, "What can I do for you?" But Michele was not smiling when she blurted out her words. On the contrary, her 15 year-old son Paul, sat motionless next to his nervous, anxious looking mother as if we were talking about the neighbor's son instead of him.

> I can't get him out of bed in the morning. I

have to literally push him out of bed into the shower and beg him to put some clean clothes on. But he prefers his jeans with self-made holes and baggy T-shirt with the motto, "The World Stinks" on it. When he stumbles in the kitchen, he seems to still be in a daze, not recognizing his father or sister. On their "Good morning, Paul," he reacts like there is little "good" to expect *that* morning and any other morning. He growls something unintelligible as if he was being transformed into a lion, and after a quick inspection of the "health food" I have prepared, he announces that he will have another Mahatma Ghandi day and refuses to eat. And then the words he has with his father! Something has to stop this battlefield!

I got the picture that it was up to me to avoid the next homicide on the block and it did not look like the suspect was going to cooperate with me. Paul could not understand all the trouble his parents were stirring up. All he wanted was to be left alone and tackle each dreary day at his own pace. He felt it was hard to get out of bed in the mornings, but given some time and space, Paul came to life around four in the afternoon. No, he did not feel like eating in the morning (too early! and who can eat while being sleepy) but he confessed to me that he snacked throughout the day on the "nutritious" goodies of the school canteen. And of course, around five o'clock in the afternoon, he was dying from hunger and raided the refrigerator, making a stack of his favorite salami sandwiches before mom came home.

> I never understood Doctor, why this boy is
> not very hungry even at night (by now it
> should be clear to her) and the only things I
> can seduce him with are spicy Chinese food
> and pizza! He hates such nutritious good-
> ies like liver, broccoli and lima beans (the
> changed, painful expression on Paul's face
> confirmed the truthfulness of this state-
> ment) but he owns the spices in the house.

Paul could hardly contain his disdain about the direction this conversation was taking. I could read it on his face.
Wasn't everyone like him? Almost everyone at school was
doing junk food except for the nerd boy next door, who came
to school with his suit and tie on. Paul was biting his dirty
nails, alternating with picking his pimples on his forehead.
"Can we change the subject please so I can get out of here to
tackle some more exciting issues in this world" reflected his
present thinking. I could see where mom's and dad's turf,
the home, easily turned into the battlefield Michele was referring to. The gawky, lean looking Paul was by no means
an easy, influenced target. But dumb he wasn't!

> You know Doctor, last week Paul was sent
> to the principal for disruptive behavior in
> the class. I really don't know what to do
> with this boy!

It turned out that Paul challenged his history teacher
regarding some facts about a battle in the second World War.
This was Paul's turf, he had read about anything about both
World Wars and he brought the facts (just the facts) over in
a style that was not appreciated by the controlling "Metal-

Teacher." Instead of allowing Paul to bring some brightness and excitement to the class discussion, the rigid teacher was insulted being provoked by what he considered "unrespectful comments" since Paul's correction of the facts brought some snickering from his fellow students. I felt for Paul. No wonder he felt bored and unchallenged, forced to follow a regimen that was good enough in the army but not in a school where he wanted to be stimulated. So Michele told me that often in class, he withdrew, sulked and refused to answer although he knew very well the solutions to the questions posed. In spite of studying very little, he managed to score eighty percent on his tests although he could easily score in the nineties if he wished. But he tells me he hates school and does not really care about good grades. On the other hand, Paul realized very well that he dominated the attention at home. A "Wood-Adolescent" senses for the first time what power he exerts over his own family members and, he especially enjoys bossing around his siblings. This "devil at home" picture is quite a contrast with the "angel at school," where he usually is elected as the class president because of his ability to involve everyone in group activities which are invariably a success.

The "Wood" prototype suffers more from adolescent acne than anyone else. It is almost like Nature pushes the irritable, angry volcano to the outside and disguises it in the form of an angry looking pimple poppy field. Of course, part of the pimples originate from the junk food he absorbs which is increasingly less assimilated by an overburdened digestive system. Often, he has an "all-gone" feeling around 11 a.m. with a steep drop in his energy. To the amazement of the parents, the ""Wood-Adolescent" starts paying attention to his exterior personal outlook. His room is still a mess, but he stays a half hour in the bathroom to comb his hair and surprises his mother with a request for a purple hairdo. And he constantly picks the blackheads in his forehead. If anything, hot in spirit and body, he is ahead of his peers to pay attention to the other sex. He is fresh with girls, gets their attention with his outrageous acts and is usually the talk of all the girls in his class. Of course, the "Wood-Adolescent" has no lack of self-confidence and knows he is smart and good-looking. While it might be an honor to anyone else to be elected as class president, once he enters his candidacy, he is sure he will be elected and finds this outcome natural as he *is* the most talented one. And it satisfies the feeling that, in no other type, is as intense as in the "Wood-Man:" the *love for power!*

I explained to Michele Paul's "make-up" and out of the corner of my eyes, I saw that Paul was following this debate with interest. By allowing the "Wood-Adolescent" to explore his curiosity and to give him enough outlets to stimulate his thinking, he has every chance in the world to grow up to be the leader and inventor he often will be in this world. He might be self-centered and refuses to obey to common rules (don't push this one in any military ruled institution) but when a parent has the patience to go with his flow, this adolescent grows up to be an exceptional human being. Of course, Paul was not going to allow me to give him a homeopathic remedy to "fix him" but being a "Liver" type myself, I could easily convince him that homeopathic Sulphur was prescribed for his acne, not to change *him*. I was not lying. There is no remedy like Sulphur to clear a stubborn adolescent acne. Two months later, his mother happily announced that her rough diamond Paul was shining now. Instead of answering with a "Yes" or "No." he pleasantly took part in every conversation, surprising the adults around him with sharp remarks and intimate knowledge of facts. He finally was living up to the potential that everyone predicted for him long before.

While the above picture is the most common among the "Wood-Liver-Boy," it should not come as a surprise that sometimes the total opposite is found. Instead of collecting worldly goods and preparing a foot long Christmas list, he might just give away everything to his friends and can't think of anything to ask for his birthday. He opts for a simple life and refuses to own anything. The classical dirty, messy boy is sometimes replaced with a fastidious young man who goes to the other extreme, although never as much as the obsessive compulsive "Earth" and "Water" types. And in certain phases of his life, he might be as loquacious as a waterfall or as silent as the deadly eye of the hurricane. No matter which "Wood-Boy" you have at home, he will certainly challenge you. But remember, unconditional support and his constitutional homeopathic remedy will do wonders to guide the family through the stormy waters ahead!

The Adult: A "True" Man

The Ambitious, Overworked Executive

> I am not here for me Doctor, but for my husband, Bruce. He has filled out your questionnaire but has no time to come on a visit himself since his work as an executive does not allow him to be here personally. And Doctor, I added here and there some-

thing, I hope you don't mind.

I did not mind. Sylvia, 44 years-old, might know her husband very well, but this short introduction was enough for me to suspect a "Wood-Liver-Man." I was not to be disappointed. His complaints were hypertension, a high cholesterol level and psoriasis, a very common angry-looking skin disease with unknown cause in Western medicine but very much linked to emotional triggering factors in alternative medicines. To the question, what happened in your life around the time these problems began, he wrote that "he had no idea."

> I think Doctor, that all his problems started around the time he went through a six month extensive, very stressful training period for this high position in his firm he now holds. It was a real stress builder for the whole family.

Sylvia, a gentle looking "Earth" type had put the finger right on the wound with the typical common sense of a down-to-earth person. In fact, the whole questionnaire was speckled with comments by her own hand-writing:

> He does not chew his food well, he eats fast, drinks with big gulps, leans back especially after meals, he loves fat, fried foods although they provoke bloating and plenty of gas.

Next to the question, "Do you weep easily and in what circumstances," he wrote: "None" followed by her comment,

"ARGH!" It looked to me as if Sylvia would not mind that her husband would show a tear here and there. And of course, "Do you have a lack of self-confidence" was followed by an expected "No." Although I had to "try" this patient in absentia, it was very easy for me to recognize the type. I asked Sylvia to tell me some more about her husband.

> Oh, he is the most popular man in the firm.
> I am not surprised he has risen to be at the
> helm of the company. Great things about
> him were predicted long time ago but
> doctor, I hardly know the man since I am in
> bed when he comes home at 11.30 p.m.,
> and I am still in bed when he leaves home
> at five in the morning. I am just worried
> about him. He does not exercise, drinks
> coffee and alcohol all day and is the
> staunchest supporter of the hamburger
> stand next to his work. I don't know how
> we managed to have three children, but he
> never has time to attend any of their soccer
> or baseball games. I am afraid for his
> health, Doctor.

Sylvia had all my sympathy. It looked to me as if Bruce was the popular guy on the block with a decreasing popularity poll at home. Married to his job, it was increasingly taking him away from home. Even when he was at home, there was no room for anyone in the family to discuss anything else but the next "billion" dollar deal in the making. Sylvia's haggard look was explained when she told me that Bruce often woke her up in the middle of the night to rehearse everything he was going to do the next day. There

was always this next "get-rich-quick-scheme," this no-miss
opportunity. Of course, most of the schemes have an unreal
touch to them. The "Wood-Man" has an entrepreneurial
quickness, a driven quality and capacity for sheer hard work,
but sometimes his promises are hollow.

> On the first date we had, Bruce over-
> whelmed me with his witty intelligence. He
> talked about any subject with such an
> authority that I listened to him in awe. He
> never talks, he *"lectures."* In fact, I remem-
> ber not saying much at all because I did not
> have a chance. He seemed to like it that I
> was listening so intently and enjoying him
> so much, but I felt I was almost listening to
> a speech. I felt flattered that he took so
> much interest in me because he was about
> the most desired bachelor in town. Every-
> thing went well, until the couple next to us
> started arguing. To my great surprise,
> Bruce jumped into the argument with both
> feet. It was there that I discovered his
> eloquence and when he returned to our
> table he said with a grin, "You know, I
> showed them who was right on this issue."
> No apologies to me, who was rather embar-
> rassed at this incident. Bruce looked like he
> loved it.

I had no doubt he did. The "Wood-Man's" favorite way
of communicating is in the form of arguments. He will join
a conversation uninvited, and makes sure he is heard. He
loves the mental stimulation and, since he is so well-in-

formed, it is hard to beat him on any given subject. A good argument allows him to diffuse all the steam bottled up in his body screaming to be let out. And he can crush the opposition with a smile, leaving them behind in shambles, but holding no personal grudge or hard feelings. This was just part of a "good" fight. Tact and diplomacy are not always high on his list. As you can see, this is the stuff of what hot shot trial lawyers are made of. They can bring the victims and their family to tears, but this is all done in the name of his conquest of giving it his all in front of the spectators. And he is not shy of telling a little white lie or making the situation a little rosier than it is. The "Wood-Man" feels that the naked truth is just that, too naked. He loves dressing it up like a beautiful lady. Bragging is part of a normal conversation. "Did you know I just started this vigorous exercise program?" he trumpets jubilantly around. Of course, his wife tells you he started walking the dog for twenty minutes twice a week. Oh, he is just following this exceptional diet: he eats anything but his beloved ice cream. All this has to assure his place on the throne, visible to everyone. Personal recognition and popularity are always on his Christmas list and he never fails to be the "groom at every wedding and the corpse at every funeral." Of course his colossal energy and great memory allow him to do five things at the same time. And he has no trouble listening to the radio and studying a project while his shouting children are running around him. He can stop reading, get up to do something else for ten minutes, and pick up exactly where he left off. Few types are able to keep that concentration. No wonder they are achievers whose curiostiy is their first and last passion. His curiosity is a certain characteristic of his vigorous intellect. But, as you have seen in Bruce, he can get burnt.

The Man Who Forgot To Stand Up For Himself

Tony was another "Wood-Man" who finally visited me because as he expressed it, "I am deprived of the quality of life I once had." He was 48 years-old and seemed to be in excellent shape otherwise.

> I guess everything started in 1987. I bought a condo that year but everything went wrong. There were major mistakes in the construction and a two year battle ensued with the contractors. At the same time, I began a new, technical, highly detailed pressured job, with long hours in a not very friendly atmosphere. To make matters worse, several alcoholics moved above my unit and were very abusive to one another in the middle of the night. I lost much sleep and my anger kept mounting. I also attended classes several nights a week and was involved in volunteer work plus I did a waiters' job on Sundays to counteract the negative work environment. I just kept pushing till the body screamed "Help."

I was almost tired just from listening to what this man went through. There is no other type in the Five Elements but the "Wood" type who could possibly have done all this at the same time for such a long time without crashing. He finally did but he expressed his chief complaint in the loss of emotional quality, rather than lack of physical endurance which I would have expected. The above situation describes another triggering factor as why somebody becomes a

"Liver-Wood-Person." His work with an abusive boss and his long-time struggle with his neighbors in which he had to suppress his anger, reflect what we call an *"indignation"* situation. With Tony, it was verbal/emotional abuse for several years for which he had no other outlet than to suppress his rage. Very often it is physical and sexual abuse leading to the same situation.

> After lunch I get tired, feel more bloating and intestinal discomfort. I feel better eating small meals more frequently. I prefer hot drinks and I dislike wind since it stirs up dust and triggers my allergies. I feel more energetic in clear, crisp temperatures. I have soft nails, which constantly split when they grow past a certain point. Then they break off. I wake up around 3 a.m. and seldom feel refreshed in the morning. At times I feel drugged or as if a truck drove over me. I crave rich, fatty, fried or spicy foods.

I explained to Tony that all those physical symptoms were related to a liver dysfunction. According to acupuncture, there were nothing but liver symptoms stemming from the continued suppressed anger over the last five years. But true to a "Wood-Man," his self-confidence was intact. Talking to me about his daily habits, he confessed that he was also a typical "Wood" super-collector. On his trips he never failed to bring back all the free pens, combs and soaps from the different hotels so that his office desk was stacked with pens and stationary paper from all over the world. He smiled when he told me that in spite of earning enough money, he would drive five miles out of his way to buy gasoline that was five cent less a gallon or to buy a two-day old loaf of bread. He found such bargains irresistible. Welcome to the family of the "Wood-Man" Tony. That is exactly what he enjoys doing. In his case, Nux Vomica, a homeopathic liver remedy, restored much of the imbalance in Tony and brought back the "joie de vivre" he was seeking.

The Oversexed "Wood-Man"

> I want to be sexual with nearly every
> woman I see, Doctor. When I am stressed, I
> try to ignore the problem, eat food, get
> busy, masturbate or sleep with women.

Fred was 36 years-old, not married and explained to me that this behavior started at age 14. At that time he masturbated continuously (it was a good feeling) while he suppressed his sexuality and had none or very little contact with girls socially. He was a wired and tense kid, who had no other outlets for relaxation but his masturbation.

> I feel a loss of personal power. I can't stop
> myself, I feel oversexed. And I am afraid I
> am abusing women sexually. I want to get
> married to my girlfriend and a sperm count
> revealed that I had too little sperm. I don't
> know how I can turn this around.

Fred looked the typical "Wood-Man:" nervous, restless, anxious about his condition, wiry and fiery, intense looking eyes. His reaction to stress was also typical: rather than checking out what the source of stress was, in a typical "Liver" fashion, he inundated the problem in getting "busy:" eating, masturbating or having sex. As I mentioned before, the hot "Wood-Man" has an increased sexual desire from a young age on. It is a way to release his tension and at the same time to express his power over other people. Very often, a "Wood-Man" is very physical in his love-making. Foreplay is done by only the most refined ones, but usually he feels just fine to "unload" his tension in a quickie without paying too much attention and consideration to the other partner's desires.He is rarely a sensual man and the act of love is less his forte then the rite of conquest. He prefers variety in his love-making, is very physical, loves rough sex, and tries out different positions which stimulate his libido; he is the moving type. After the sexual act, he gets up immediately, goes to the toilet and keeps busy going on with whatever comes to his mind. He is very passionate in general and wants to move fast in a relationship; it's all or nothing in his eyes. This is not so much because of desire to strong commitment but rather to have the admiring attention, the possession of yet another "treasure." He loves to have a beautiful woman around him but in reality, that comes on the same line as a beautiful car, a nice home, an exciting career, etc. It is again his sense of collecting that drives this "Wood-Man" rather than true feelings of appreciation and intimacy. At the same token, more than any other type, he will be inclined to have a one-night stand. This is linked to his lack of commitment and fear for new situations with lasting responsibilities. Murders committed in the heat of passion are usually committed by this "Liver" type. It is natural for the "Wood-Man" to make up after an argument by forcing sex upon his partner. Or to come home after a busy, tense day to have sex just to "relax" him. Other "triggering" factors to sex are vacation trips, after a great physical effort or while dancing which stimulates him erotically. His favorite erogenic zones are the thighs, neck and knee crease. The "Wood" type is more physical than other types, has more stamina and thrives on explosive, short-lasting feats like sex and sports to balance himself. In spite of all the self-confidence he exudes, the "Wood-Man" is rather anxious and hypernervous before the sexual act. This leads easily to ejaculatio praecox or loss of sperm before penetration.

I have read books about serial murders who committed their acts out of rage towards women becaused they were laughed at at an earlier age because of their ejaculatio praecox. Link this to the already explosive behavior of the "Wood-Man" and the potential of violence is great. If the relationship sours, he has little difficulty packing up and going on with his life. No grudges are held against the ex-partner, no dwelling over the past. Rather, he moves on and explores new exciting people. Fred had four relationships before the last one, all of them of short duration. But his complaints were still self-centered: no word about how his aggressive, sexual behavior might have hurt the other party. He will not understand how a "Water" type can suffer so much from a broken heart. His lack of tolerance to remain sympathetic is expressed by "Why don't you move on with your life," or "Get a life, will you."

Fred's low sperm count was not a coincidence. Five thousand years ago the Chinese called this loss of spermatic Qi or Energy through "Affairs of the Bedroom." In that time, it was very common for the emperors, to sleep with many women throughout their life. Most of them did not live beyond 45. There was one exception. The Yellow Emperor, who lived beyond 90, had at his court a woman adviser called the Pure Lady. The art of bedroom affairs became a well-established branch of Chinese medicine whose ideas were mainly derived from this famous Yellow Emperor (2698 BC) in his conversations with the Pure Lady. The Yellow Emperor had a total of more than 1,000 women in his palace. For him, sex was like the three legged stool: a triple purpose of ensuring the continuity of the human race, satisfying his personal sexual desire and achieving personal longevity. The latter he achieved by having intercourse with as many as ten young women a day, *without ejaculating*, while capturing their orgasm.

The most damaging effect of intercourse for the man is the act of ejaculation, because each ejaculation will cost him some precious Kidney Energy, eventually depriving him of sex power (low sperm count followed by impotence). The Chinese compare sexual intercourse to an act between an obedient nice mare and a dominating dragon, symbol of heaven, fire and Yang. The key for the man is to not get over excited and reach his orgasm too soon or he will be merely a non-active participant, losing his energy without capturing the woman's energy through her orgasm. This phenomenon is described in homeopathy as "Never well since loss of fluids." These fluids refer not only to blood and plasma, but also to sperm. Rather than considering *excessive* masturbation as something innocent, it can and often lead to low sperm count and impotence!

The Ragged Philosopher

I don't know why I come here, Doctor. I guess it is because my wife Linda insists on it. She tells me I have become an old hack,

> continuously complaining and bickering.
> She says she wants to lock me up in my
> room so she does not have to listen to my
> negativity.

John, 67 years-old, looked the role of the burnt-out philosopher. His shirt, bearing the spots of the spaghetti sauce of the previous day, was hanging out of his pants. His socks were mismatched, and in spite of the chilly day, John had no need for an overcoat. With his hair sticking out in all directions and sporting a three day old beard, he looked at me in a bored fashion, probably thinking about what kind of a doctor I was in which his wife had so much faith.

> As far I am concerned, Doctor, the world
> stinks. Our politicians are no good, no one
> wants to do anything in this world for
> someone else without expecting something
> back fivefold. Children are ungrateful
> morons. And frankly, this world pisses me
> off so much that I don't want to have any
> part of it. Can you blame me for that
> Doctor?

This was the same John I had known for twenty years: an ambitious go-getter, always on the run and dealing and wheeling with whoever wanted to listen to him. But he was always a "Wood-Man." He was very critical, sarcastic, and belligerent, in short, a man of "bilious temper." His anxiety and nervousness was tied up inside of him, ready to explode whenever needed. He could not stand small talk and would walk away from it without apologizing. In fact, he would often interrupt you and voice his criticism (usually shouts) before turning his back to you. Frequently this "Wood-Man" *is* everything he accuses others of not being—clear thinking, educated in almost every subject, philosophical, hardworking, and fast-acting. His wife told me that he would explode in traffic when a car cut in ahead of him while at the same time he would turn a cold shoulder to her suggestion that they had taken a wrong turn. Of course, when they were lost, it was the fault of the government for not giving clear enough directions. But all these years of hard-living changed John from a brilliant, domineering subject into a tearful misanthrope who was always angry and who was just as much run down physically as mentally. The "Wood-Man," usually a very intelligent individual with a sharp quick wit, becomes difficult to live with and especially bad-humored upon awaking in the morning. He might lose interest in newspapers ("Nothing but lies in those damn papers!") and when he goes to a concert or speaking event, he will fall asleep to demonstrate his outrage at such nonsense. "That's nothing new to me, " he will say. And he checks out to the despair of his wife. The bright candle, once flickering with such intensity, has been burned from both ends. All this "Wood-Man" wants is to be left alone. He becomes a haughty, dictatorial loner who can't sleep and is mentally and physically exhausted. He is disorganized and confused, indifferent to things material and physical. He will not express his feelings but rather intellectualizes them so as to disqualify their importance. Again this "end stage" of a "Wood-Man" can easily be avoided if there is a homeopathic intervention earlier on when his "do-or-die" behavior is recognized and remedied.

His wife Linda did not have to commit a homicide for John did listen with interest to what I had to say about his situation. ("Wood-Men" always want to hear a "scientific," no-nonsense explanation.) A subsequent dose of Sulphur 10M, constitutional, brought happiness in his life again. He stayed critical, but turned his continuous negativity into volunteer work, organizing raffles and parties, and found himself back in the limelight. There was one difference. He could look at himself with much better perspective and became a grinning, good-natured fellow anyone could count on.

You have met some different shades of "Wood-Liver" men. I am sure you recognize plenty of them among your family and friends. To summarize them emotionally:

The "Wood-Man"
Intelligent, hard worker, irritable, impatient, decision taker, witty, philosophical, high sex-drive, selfish, untidy, collector, sportive, quarrelsome, creative, great memory, passionate, violent, zealous, inspiring, enthusiastic, logical, sharp-tongued, authoritarian, ambitious, great strategist and good provider.

Classical examples are generals like Napoleon Bonaparte, George C. Patton, Erwin Rommel and Heinz Guderian who all discarded old-fashioned war tactics. They introduced speed and surprise ("Blitz-krieg!") which reflected their own "Liver" metabolism. They were ahead of their time in bringing their own energy over to the masses of the army and ushering us into modern times ahead of schedule. But among all the well-known generals, General Douglas A. MacArthur was *the* prototype of the Wood-Liver" man. His own aide, Colonel Enoch Crowder, said, "Douglas Mac Arthur is the most flamboyantly egotistical man I have ever met." To the Filipinos he was a hero and inspired leader who captured their imagination with his dramatic flair. At any given moment he was visible on a throne, just as when he waded through the ocean setting foot again on Filipino soil. He even did it twice just to accomodate the press. His own rhetoric, his personal attitudes were the strongest guidelines in his decisions. But, with disregard to his own safety, he never lacked courage.

In what other professions do you often find "Liver-Wood" men?

High-powered litigation lawyers are this type. They like to argue, think fast under pressure, stick to the facts ("Just the facts, ma'am!"), although they are able to make them more colorful according to their needs. They like finding mistakes, digging up and investigating secrets. They are usually highly career-and work-oriented and deal with stress by taking on *more* work. Often they are much more successful in their professional world than their personal one where they miss basking in the glory and attention they receive at work (unless of course they are married with someone compatible according to the Laws explained in Chapter One). They need to marry someone who can listen to them, admire them and most often agree with what they think and do. An "Earth-Woman" or "Water-Woman" are most suitable for them. The first one is contend with an uneventful life at home, the latter has too many fears and anxieties and admires her husband, who seems to be very comfortable in the limelight of the public.

Other "Wood-Men" often are inventors, mechanics, scholars, politicians, editors, journalists, non-fiction writers (World War books, *Guinness Book of Records, The People's Almanac*, etc.),radio personalities, TV anchors, realtors, car salesmen, brokers and high-powered executives. A "Wood-Man" can be a great homeopathic physician with his flair of non-conformism. He does not stick to the rules, and is seduced by the strict scientific basis of homeopathy. He is mostly sharp-minded and highly critical of the hit-and-miss methods of modern medicine. He loves the amount of study and work necessary in order to become a good homeopathic physician. He is able to focus sharply on each patient individually without throwing out names and catalogues of diseases. His patient is always unique.

The Physical Give-Aways And Clues Of The "Wood-Man"

If you had any trouble recognizing your "Wood-Man," there are many physical characteristics which will make a Sherlock Holmes out of every woman who wants to size up the men in her life.

If the "Wood-Man" takes you out to dinner, don't expect a "New Age" restaurant. He loves fried and fatty foods, spicy, sour and highly seasoned, topped off with a good glass of beer and a sweet dessert with coffee. In other words: as with the rest of his life, he wants to be stimulated by his food too. He does not care much about its presentation and gobbles it up in the shortest time possible. Although he could be a vegetarian, he loves meat (especially lamb) and proclaims it gives him energy. His highly strung nature makes the "Wood-Man" burn this food fast although incompletely. He loosens his belt after meals because there is often immediate bloating, especially below the navel. Belching, hiccups and passing gas are on the menu of every "Wood-Man," to the despair of his neighbor. He cannot skip a meal: this easily provokes hypoglycemia, another Liver sign. Whenever he goes too long without eating, he gets dizzy, lightheaded, sweaty, headachy and feels he needs to eat immediately or he will pass out. He poorly tolerates onions, beans and oysters, which only increase his gas production. Often he has classic perspiration, the odor of onions.

He is the first prototype to succumb to drug and alcohol indulgences: he is, in general, the addiction-prone personality. He invariably tends to take medicinal and street drugs, using them to support his bad life style habits and to change his moods.from the ups and downs he is experiencing. He is the classical student who starts taking coffee and mood-elevators when he is too tired to study. Before he knows it, he is caught in a vicious cycle: stimulating drugs and food during the days, ever-stronger sleeping pills during the night. A hang-over is part of a good evening out, but the next day causes him continuous heartburn and indigestion. All this jerking around of his metabolism leads to typical constipation: a frequent and ineffectual desire for stool but passing little at a time. There is an urge for some time before action takes place. Then he has the impression that there is some faeces left in the rectum. No wonder so many "Wood-Men" suffer from hemorrhoids and painful bleeding anal cuts or fissures.

The eyes are related to the "Liver" function. Often this type has big, penetrating, even menacing, eyes. Cold, staring, blue-steeled eyes reflect the inner soul of the "Wood-Man." When you look at the eyes, you note that one eye is more open than the other. The left eye corresponds to everything that is personal, to the person himself. The right eye is what that person shows the world. For instance, if the right eye is smaller than the left one, it shows that this person is very careful and suspicious. A criminal will have a smaller right eye: he hides from the world. If the left eye is smaller, it means that this person will be very private and hides his personal affairs. The "Wood-Man" usually has straight eyebrows: they belong to a person who has his head in the right place and who loves logical reasoning. Often he has very thick eyebrows reflecting his great influence and strong will on other people. But eyes often become a place of weakness resulting in tearing of the eyes due to allergies, floaters in the eyes, migraines with flashing lights in the eyes, and blurred vision requiring constant change of prescription glasses. The nails are also under the domain of this organ. Depending on the strength of the Liver, they have strong or very frail nails that peel off easily and do not grow. The white spots on the nails show a lack of silica. This person often will have dental trouble. If you see a man who has premature gray hair, it's a dead give-a-way that he is a "Wood-Man!"

The "Wood-Man" really should sleep alone. He will easily wake up around 3 a.m. with a restless mind, rehearsing what to do the next day or trying to compose another of his never-fail schemes. After 3 a.m. he tosses around in bed, throws the blankets off or sticks his feet out from under the blankets. Of course he wakes up unrefreshed and in a foul mood. He will be very sensitive to noise: don't put the music on, don't even talk to him before he has gulped a couple cups of coffee. He can suffer from morning sneezing attacks, occipital headaches and migraines caused by too much rich and fatty food eaten the previous day. If he happens to stick out his tongue, take advantage of it. A red-purple tongue, especially on the sides, gives you another invaluable clue: only a "Wood-Man" has this! His favorite color: green-blue and its shades.

The "Wood-Man" and His Diseases

Amazingly enough, you can predict the diseases from which this prototype will suffer. It is like "Tell me who you are, and I will tell you what your health problems are going to be." Or you can turn it around. "Tell me about your diseases, and I tell you who you are!" Knowing what the men in your life suffer from is a confirmation of their constitution. I think it is a great advantage for a woman who marries a "Wood-Man," and for that man himself, to know what the kinks in his armor are. With the help of supplements and homeopathic remedies, many of these diseases can be avoided.

As mentioned above, the eye is a reflection of the Liver function. Any condition of the eye, burning, tearing (in hay fever), bleeding in the retina, blurred vision, floaters, glaucoma, conjunctivitis, double vision, is an expression of a deranged liver function. Don't expect a liver test to confirm this. I am talking about liver changes taking place long before any sensitive blood test can pick this up. There are exceptions. Cataracts of the eye is related more to a deficient Kidney function. One of the functions of the Liver is to *store the blood*. It supplies blood to the muscles and tendons during movement and exercise. Hence, if there is deficient blood stored (the reasons are explained further), the "Wood-Man" will suffer from cramps and painful spasms. One of these "modern diseases" is fibromyositis or fibromyalgia," which is *not* a disease but a simple expression of disturbed Liver function. Other muscular symptoms will also reflect this: tremors, fasciculations (crude tremors of big muscle groups) and twitching of the eyes. True thyroid trouble with goiter formation and weight loss is also a constitutional "Wood" disorder. Allergies in general, and especially to insect bites, pollen, the sun, medications with hives mean liver trouble.

Conditions related to the life style of the "Wood-Man" are stomach ulcers, cirrhosis of the liver, hypertension, insomnia with waking up between 1- 3 a.m., nausea, indigestion, hemorrhoids, constipation, gall bladder attacks with stone formation, bloating below the navel and hypoglycemia. The "Wood-Man" also suffers from a certain form of arthritis: the pain *changes* from one joint to another, appearing and disappearing quickly.

The "Wood-Man" a has fear of heights, narrow places, tunnels and a susceptibility to motion sickness (especially car and sea).

In general, we can say that a "Wood-Man" usually has robust health as long as he keeps himself in balance. His energy and stamina are superior to anyone else's in the five constitutions and, coupled with his perseverance and determination, few obstacles will stand in his way. If he suffers from a disease, it will be in style with his whole being: a strong, sudden, fulminant disease from which he will recover or deteriorate quickly, depending on his course of action.

How Did He Become a "Wood-Man?"

Your understanding of a "Wood-Man" and your ability to polish this diamond in the rough at the same time will be improved by answering this question. No doubt, many of them were born that way. Often my patients say, I am just like my father, inquisitive, scholarly, hot tempered and an achiever. These are the true "Wood" constitutions. However, many times in life, certain events will add a "layer of Wood" to your constitution (whatever it may be). Patients have repeatedly said to me, "I recognize myself now being a "Wood-Man" but as a child I was truly a "Water-Man." What changed him or added this layer?

By far the most common factor is continuous anger and rage. Whoever is trapped in a situation which evokes anger and frustration is bound to add many "Wood" signs to their constitution. One form of anger is especially prevalent: *suppressed* anger from suffering an *indignation* situation. It is a sad fact of modern life that spousal abuse, either sexual, verbal, emotional or physical, is on the rise. While females are prime victims, many males are abused and neglected, often as children. When their dignity is taken away, most children react by withdrawing into their own world. These suppressed feelings often reemerge later during therapy, throwing these victims into a spiral of despair and ill health. I remember such a case.

> Doctor, I am here because of my 7 year-old adopted son, Marc. We adopted him at age 3. Originally, he showed almost "autistic behavior." He would shout a lot when I would change his diapers. Later, he became hyperactive and was put on Ritalin. But what my husband and I can't deal with is his recent sexually inappropriate behavior. He stuck his finger in the vagina of his 2 year-old cousin and I saw him rubbing his penis on his 20 month-old brother.

Barbara looked very sad and tired when she told me this

story. Modern tests were performed with negative results.
A psychiatrist diagnosed him with "Impulse control disorder, attention deficit, hyperactive disorder and post trau-
matic stress disorder." In my opinion the psychiatrist missed
the boat. These "diagnoses" were just descriptions of his
present status and did not explain *why* he exhibited this behavior. But it became clear to me as Barbara continued her
story.

> Marc's natural mother was pregnant with
> him at age 15. She herself was sexually
> abused by her stepfather and her natural
> mother for years. As a child Marc was
> sexually abused and emotionally neglected.
> In fact, he has a recurrent dream of some-
> body hurting him in the rectum. He shows
> very little emotion about anything. I never
> know what he feels.

These were the clues to his behavior. His natural mother
was sexually abused while pregnant with him. That alone
would have been sufficient to produce a child with this behavior. In such a case, at birth the child needs the same homeopathic remedy as the mother needed while pregnant
with him. To make matters worse, the poor child was abused
himself, which was like being hit twice with the same
trauma. This child never had a chance. His behavior should
be diagnosed as "Never well since sexual abuse and abandonment." His only salvation can come from therapy aimed
at that issue. His medical diagnoses (sexual deviant behavior, attention deficit disorder and emotional flatness) are *consequences*. Treating these end results, rather than the true leak-
age of energy, or the real triggering factor can never lead to

recovery. It only will add drug pictures to his disease picture which is exactly what happened. In this case, the homeopathic remedy, Staphysagria, covered his symptoms well and should lead to considerable improvement. This is the picture of the restless, active, violent, sexual "Wood-Man." In this case, if not corrected, the child could easily get into trouble with the law because of rape or even murder.

Indignation is not the only factor leading to a "Wood-Man" picture. There is also *disappointment*. Setbacks in professional life (i.e. not receiving a well-deserved promotion, getting rejections [for film actors], non-acknowledgment of good performance while someone else receives the accolades) or simply disappointment in his children are all possible scenarios leading to a "Wood" situation. In other words, the Liver has to take the brunt of this insult, leading to a host of apparently unrelated illnesses. I remember a classical example of Chronic Fatigue Syndrome in a well-known actor, Andre.

> Dr. Luc, I can't remember my lines. My
> mind goes blank, I look stupid and my film
> director is fed up with me. All this has
> taken a toll on me. I am anxious, feel
> extremely fatigued, wake up in the morn-
> ing with sore muscles and my mood
> swings drive me crazy. My blood tests
> show the presence of all these viruses, but I
> can't understand why this is happening to
> me.

This is not surprising. Most patients do not make the connection between what happened in their life and the onset of the disease. They are too wrapped up in the physician's end result. After some gentle probing, I found out that Andre's health started to decline after the biggest disappointment in his life. He was nominated for an Oscar Award with everyone predicting he would win. It meant a lot to him because it was a way of proving to his mother that he was a success in the world. When he did not win he went in shock. He slept for three days and has never been well since. Andre resembles the case of the burnt-out "Wood-Man," John, the ragged philosopher. Yet, a disappointment remedy, in his case Lycopodium, restored another case of CFIDS.

Other situations leading to a "Wood-Man" are being humiliated (vexation), mortification or a big fright, continuous frustration, substance abuse, alcohol misuse and legal drug overuse so common in our modern world.

Causality of the "Wood-Man"

Anger (especially suppressed), indignation, frustration, disappointment, irritability, humiliation, drug-alcohol use, fright.

Supplements and Homeopathic Remedies to Balance the "Wood-Man"

Some of the homeopathic remedies have been mentioned already. One remedy will excel: Sulphur, the great cleansing remedy. Many of the patients described above have benefited from Sulphur in a constitutional dose. Another one is Nux Vomica, the remedy for the fast modern life with its stress, fast food and drugs.

The reader should not decide on his own homeopathic remedy. A well-trained homeopathic physician is the only one who can truly turn things around with what he calls the "simillimum." This is nothing more than the remedy which *exactly* fits your situation. There are several other homeopathic remedies such as *Carduus* and *Chelidonium* which strengthen a weakened liver. Other big remedies are Magnesium Muriaticum (CFIDS since hepatitis), Lycopodium for the "Liver" type who lost self-confidence and Staphysagria for the indignation situation. Allium Cepa and Euphrasia are the leaders for hay fever. While the physician should assist you with the choice of remedy, the above described situations will enable you to decide, with your physician, what remedy the man in your life needs.

What every reader *can* do immediately is to support and polish the "Wood-Man" through readily available supplements. A must for every "Wood-Man" is *Milk thistle or Silymarin.* It is Nature's answer for an abused, sluggish and toxic liver. This herbal compound is believed to offset damage that can result from chemical abuse and environmental pollutants. Liver damage is caused primarily by toxins that create free radicals in liver tissue. Free radicals are highly reactive components that cause damage to other molecules and cells. Sylimarin's potent antioxidant action prevents the formation of free radicals in the liver, thereby helping to reduce the potential for damage. In addition, because of its unique ability to stimulate protein synthesis, Silymarin stimulates the formation of new liver cells. Take two tablets daily.

For anyone who has abused his liver, especially with alcohol, a *Vitamin B complex*, which includes Vitamin B1 or thiamin, Vitamin B6 and Folic Acid will be indispensable. Alcohol abuse leads to deficiency of these important vitamins. Take two a day.

Zinc is called the "health-protecting mineral." Even mild deficiency can lead to a low sperm count (important for the high-sexed "Wood-Man" in general, who loses zinc with each ejaculation). Moderate deficiencies lead to retarded growth, poor appetite, mental lethargy, slow wound healing and night blindness. The latter occurs because zinc is needed to transport the Vitamin A to the retina of the eye. Furthermore, "If you drink, take zinc." Heavy drinkers lose a lot of zinc in their urine. A zinc deficiency also leads to general hair loss. It is easy to spot zinc deficiency on the nails. White spots alert you to the need to replenish your deficient zinc stores. You should take a zinc tablet that provides you with about 50 mg *elemental* zinc daily. Zinc is one of the remedies available for prostrate problems. Its specific need is characterized by the man who can only urinate, or urinates easier, when *he is sitting on the toilet.* Also, his prostrate problem is aggravated by *wine intake.*

Another important element is *Gingko Biloba.* The gingko tree is native to China and Japan but has been transplanted around the world as a decorative tree. The root bark of gingko and the leaves are used to extract chemical compounds, called *flavonoids.* One of these flavonoids, quercetin, has anti-allergy effects. It is a natural antihistamine preparation which does not cause severe drowsiness. In fact, the anti-asthmatic action of ginko biloba is one of its main traditional uses in China. Use three capsules daily. For strengthening of the nails use *Silicea,* two tablets daily. There is no doubt that the "Wood-Man" will suffer from a variety of muscular disorders including fatigue, cramps, spasms, tears or sprains. He will benefit greatly from a daily dose of Magnesium/Calcium in a ratio of 2 to 1. For instance, 2,000 mg of Mg combined with 1,000 mg of Ca.

By determining the right homeopathic remedy and supplying the "Wood-Man" with the above mentioned supplements, you should be able to see him change as a whole person, mentally, physically and emotionally. All this will lead to a longer and healthier life span and above all, a companion who will be strong, faithful, determined, intelligent, even-tempered and creative!

FOUR

The Fire-Heart Man

The Child : A Charming Actor

> This is Thomas, Doctor. Isn't he darling? He
> is a very popular child at school. But his
> teacher tells me he is too playful and does
> not pay attention. He is the class clown and
> acts out the scenes of the history teacher. At
> home he can drive me crazy, too. He plays
> tricks on me. I think he is not at home, but
> he hides under his bed and does not an-
> swer my calls. And he thinks it is funny!

Looking at Thomas, her 7 year-old son, he seemed to be
having lots of fun. Obviously, he enjoyed being the center of
attention, smiled graciously at me and did not seem in the
least embarrassed. He was a tall lad, appealing in his openness. His big eyes and easy smile would win anyone's heart
and I could see that his mother was no match for him. The
"Heart-Boy" is all joy. Work becomes play, punishment is
easily shaken off as a minor inconvenience. In fact, Thomas'
mother told me it drove her crazy that when he was sent to
his room as punishment, he would whistle and sing as if
nothing had happened. A "Heart-Boy" bears no resentment
to anyone.

> He is popular all right. Everyone wants to
> be around his clowning and imagination.
> Even when it is obvious that he is lying it's

hard to be angry at him. He has such an
appealing, interesting way that you almost
have to laugh at his fantasies. Whenever his
friends want a good time, they turn to him.
He always finds ways to entertain them
and to get himself into trouble.

The "Heart-Boy" is not as much a leader as the "Liver-Boy." The latter, through his knowledge of facts, his enthusiasm and stamina, and his ambition and competitiveness, secures for himself the "desired" position of leader. The "Heart-Boy" is just fun to be around. He is usually an agreeable, unassertive child. He tells little white lies with great ebullience. But there is no drive for him to be an imposing figure among his peers. He loves to please everyone, which is not difficult, and is usually friends with everyone. It is the child with whom no one is angry. He is always the first to volunteer for a play at school. For him there is no better reward than the applause of his fellow students. He is the dominant figure on stage, always dead center where he catches the most attention. He definitely does not have the energy of a "Wood-Boy," but he more than makes up for it by his need to be admired and shine on stage. He is the one who performs even when too sick to do so because the applause of his fellow students refuels his energy. Once the play is over, he will collapse with a smile, knowing that his performance was superb and that he was center stage again. Of course, he is the boy who loves to take acting classes. From a young age on, he will show some talent as a stand-up comedian with dead-pan expressions. His whole world is a stage. You will never know if what he says is true or if he is playing a trick on you with an outrageous lie. He looks so innocent with those big eyes staring at you that he must be telling the truth. Watch out! The more innocent he looks, the guiltier he can be.

Since he is not ambitious, he does not care much about getting good grades. It is not that he lacks intelligence; far from it. His excellent memory often helps him through hardships, but he is not a collector of facts. Quite the opposite of the "Wood-Boy" who loves "facts," the "Heart-Boy" loves using his imagination. History and geography are favorite subjects. They allow him to travel freely in his dreams to foreign countries and to play the valiant knight rescuing the darling princess on one of his crusades. Let him write a dissertation about fiction and he stands out. Other subjects at school bore him. Not because they are too easy, as is the case for the"Wood-Boy," but because he quickly loses interest. The exactness and coldness of sciences like math, physics and chemistry do not appeal to him since they leave no room for self-expression. He is so easily distracted and has so little physical and mental stamina, that he drifts off to his dream world, leaving the security of figures in math to the "Earth-Boys," who love exact, uneventful things in their life.

Oh yes, he is very impressionable and wildly enthusiastic about new undertakings. But rarely does he finish a task. He can be easily enthused about a project today, and toss it out the very next one because something more exciting came along. We call them "good beginners, bad finishers." It is their lack of stamina that kills a lot of their projects. He darts around like a butterfly, always on the move, as if every moment is the last one he will have. There is a frenzy in every move as if they know they won't be able to keep it up. While the "Wood-Boy" has almost no fears, the "Heart-Boy" with his wild imagination has plenty! Some of the most outspoken ones are his fears of the dark (they always want to sleep with a night light), of being alone, of lightning and thunderstorms and of spiders. He loves to be consoled, to be hugged and kissed and he will lie still anytime for a little massage. None of this appeals to the "Wood-Boy" who looks at this behavior as being "girlish." No other type in the five proto-types has as much anima (or Yin-female) in a man as the "Heart-Boy."

As 7 year-old Thomas was leaving my office with his mother, he winked at me to show his approval of the enjoy-able moments we spent together. Of course, the talk was all about him. He had made friends with my whole staff through his innocent good looks and his unbridled curios-ity, and now it was time to move on to other exciting things. No one would dream of taking away any of his very ap-pealing characteristics. In his case, the homeopathic rem-edy was Phosphorus. It increased his stamina, and made him finish many of the projects he had shelved a long time ago. His playfulness had some firmness to it and his fears abated greatly under the gentle action of the remedy. I guess he will always remain one of my favorite patients.

The Teenager: Confused and Humorist

As they grow into teenagers, not much changes except maybe their growing concern with their looks. Looks be-come very important and even boys will spend consider-able time in the bathroom, to the chagrin of other family members. There is always one more hair that did not fall into place or the color of their shirt does not match the rest of the outfit. The "Heart-Teenager," enjoying nearly every-thing that comes his way, has this slight grin he always wears. He is the class president, friendly with everyone and immensely popular. He is voted the "most likely to succeed" in life by his peers, reflecting more a skewed opinion by his friends than reality. It is not difficult for a "Heart-Teenager" to exude a lot of self confidence. But, unlike the "Wood-Teenager," this self-confidence is not based on what he is achieving in school but, rather, on what he should be able to achieve *if* he was not dreaming and playing his life away.

As they age, they are as much a victim of their sensitiveness as younger peers. Their illnesses might be more profound but that does not deter them from being cheerful. The next case from my clinic confirms that.

> I am consulting for my son, Regis, a 16 year-old. He is busy rehearsing a play at school but he managed to fill out your questionnaire. I filled out one more elaborate version for him. He suffers from Chronic Fatigue Syndrome and is constantly fatigued and nauseated. Also, he has poor concentration, headaches and is sensitive to chemicals and foods. He loves to visit the malls with his friends, but he always gets sick there. It sometimes makes him sad and depressed as he feels that he must be "weird" to be like this.

Was this another "incurable" case of CFIDS or was there more to it? Johanna, his mother, proceeded to tell me more about the center of her worries.

> You know, Doctor, I blame myself. When Regis was born, we lived in Papua, New Guinea. I had to take anti-malaria medications and was exposed to chemical spray-

ing while being pregnant with him, and,
again, while breast feeding him. I always
thought this had something to do with his
illness now.

While the meaning of this incident was obscure at the
time, it became a lot clearer as his mother and I reviewed
Regis' "time-line:" all the events in his life, physical and
emotional.

Regis himself started taking anti-malaria
medication at age one. He witnessed me
having a grand-mal seizure at age four and
was very distressed about it. At age 8 his
father worked in the Middle East and was
absent for two years. Regis missed him a
lot. At age 13, he was exposed to chemical
sprays at the primary school and got severe
hay fever. At age 14, he started high school
in brand new buildings. In fact the buildings were still under construction while the
students were present. Immediately after
this he caught a "cold" which never went
away. He has never been the same since
and now has all these symptoms for which
he has been diagnosed as Chronic Fatigue.

It was obvious to me that Regis was a sensitive boy. Emotionally, in the way he reacted to his mother's illness and
his father's absence, but also in the way his disease had finally come to a head. While the first incident of spraying
and subsequent emotional traumas had not translated into
any illness, his hay fever at age 13 was the first sign of a

broken defense. And the third exposure, this time to fumes and building materials at his new high school, was too much for an already predisposed and susceptible constitution. It caved in under the same repeated offenses since early childhood and he was never the same. Could this have been avoided? No doubt! If Regis would have taken a homeopathic remedy to offset the bad effects of exposure to chemicals and medications, his constitution would have been fortified enough to avoid his hay fever and CFIDS. I had no doubt about his "Heart-Personality" when I read his version of the questionnaire. He was very funny.

On some questions, he wrote: "I just told you that, didn't you listen?" On the question, "What happens when you fast?," this sharp-witted guy wrote: "It's silly to miss meals so I don't do it." On his favorite drink: "Tequila Slammer. No, not really. It's definitely not veggie juice, anyway." On vaccinations received: "Ask Mom, it's her fault." On perspiration: "Yes, and did you know that we perspire 2.5 liters a day without exercise? On sunshine: "I like to wear my sunnies a lot. And they were only $9, too. Cool." On his nails and hair: "They are gorgeous, lover, and quite strong but bendy. My hair, sweetie, is oily at the roots." On previous operations: "Yes, I had a nose job and my cheek bones are rearranged and liposuction and...Oh, sorry, what was the question again? Um no, I haven't." On the position in which he slept: "I mean when you sleep you don't really notice what position you are in, do you? Do you?" On how he wakes up in the morning: "Every morning I bounce out of bed to do 500 sit-ups, 50 push-ups, 100 pull-ups and two hours of aerobics. No, not really! I crawl out of bed and whisper good morning to the cat." If he likes consolation: "I wish 1-555-CONFIDE was a real number so I could ring up the Beatles and have a good whine occasionally." On his self-confidence: "Many people think I am actually quite full of it. My first girlfriend dropped me after three days saying I was full of myself." About his family history: "Why not ask them?" I laughed as I read. But at the same time there was no doubt about his constitutional remedy: he was light-hearted in spite of a serious illness, answered my questions with intelligence and sharp humoristic replies, and underneath showed the great sensitivity and warmth of a "Heart-Man." His CFIDS disappeared with a Phosphorus 10M dose. But what a character. I think he will go on to become the next Robin Williams!

The "Heart-Man:" the Sensitive Soul

The Universal Reactor

You know, Doctor, life is not worth living any more. I can't leave this apartment because everything in the world is killing me. Fumes, fabrics, cigarette smoke, ink from a newspaper, molds, perfumes, even the TV screen and my computer screen. I have become allergic to this world, Doctor. I can't have my friends over for fear that they will wear something I will react to and frankly, I feel embarrassed to always tell them not to do this, not to wear that...

I visited, Frank, 54 years-old, in his apartment at the request of his sister. Frank looked remarkably young and cheerful for his age despite this colossal disease. His whole apartment, located on the 29th floor, was stripped to the bare minimum. Everything was linen and cotton, and a piano was the center of the living room. His sister brought him food once a day, but beyond that, his socializing was almost non-existent. He spent his days playing his own sad compositions on the piano. They were songs reflecting the loss of his life, and while he was playing for me (the eternal actor!), he had tears in his eyes. But playing for me had its healing purpose. Very rarely did he have a sympathetic audience and his raw, deep voice reflected very much the darkness of his most inner soul, a loss of life and longing for those beautiful, cherished moments, a long time ago in his life. As he was telling me his story, I thought how frightful it was that this could happen to anyone. But above all, any "Heart-Man" or "Heart-Woman" would be the one most susceptible to this trauma.

> I was only 26 when my life changed. I was involved in a major car accident. I had broken many bones and was hospitalized for six months. I received tons of medications: antibiotics for the multiple operations I needed, sleeping pills, painkillers; all this for someone who had never taken medications until that time. When I left the hospital, my bones were healed but I was a wreck. I had become sensitive and allergic to the whole world. I am 54 years-old now, and I have not been outside of this room since I was 26. My wife left me because she could not deal with this life. I can't blame her. My doctors abandoned me declaring me a mental case.

A frightful story indeed. And not a rare one anymore. I have seen plenty of these patients and their numbers are growing. While most of you might not know anyone like this, almost anyone has a friend or family member who reacts violently to perfumes, cigarette smoke or gasoline fumes. Even "mass" reactions are possible. I remember one incident in Santa Monica, California where 150 school children, visiting a theater, became instantly ill. Eminent doctors labeled it as a case of "mass-hysteria." What an insult to these victims. Later it was reported that the theater they visited, had been freshly painted that same morning. I have no doubt that many of those teenagers were "Heart-Persons" and they reacted to the fumes of the paints. But the medical response reflects the standpoint of the medical community in general: if most of us can live in this world, then those who exhibit those innumerable reactions are, to say the least, mental cases! Shame on those doctors who don't recognize the different types of patients and would prefer to put everyone into their little classifications, not to the benefit of the patient, but because of the laziness and arrogance of these all-mighty physicians.

Not all "Heart-People" will show sensitivity to such an extreme degree as Frank does. But, in general, we can say that the sensitivity in the "Heart-Man" runs through all his planes: physical, spiritual and mental. We can call this "Heart-Man" the human barometer. He is highly sensitive to electrical changes in the air. Often he will experience a dull headache and general fatigue before a storm breaks out. He will feel a change of weather long before the TV weather person has voiced an opinion and with much more accuracy. I have already named some of the more common sensitivities this man experienced. It is also peculiar that most of his reactions are to the exterior world, and less to foods (the latter is the case for the "Water-Man"). More than any other type, he will react to odors, strong light, noise and changes in temperature. He is the man who will get the "Sick Building Syndrome." His sensitivity to different building materials and lights in his work place is so great that he will come down with an array of illnesses, most frequently recurrent colds, headaches and chronic fatigue. The "Heart-Man" also has another problem. His sensitivity extends, of course, to drugs, especially anesthesia. He is the patient who will stay "asleep" under anesthesia longer than anyone else, much to the surprise of the anesthesiologist, who has trouble "waking this patient up" after an operation. Anyone who has an "out-of-the-body" experience under anesthesia is a "Heart-Person." His sensitivity also extends to the spiritual and mental plane since the "Heart-Man" is like a psychogenic sponge soaking in the whole environment. The "Heart-Man" has great clairvoyance and intuition. He feels and sees with his heart. He is the seer and prophet. His dreams can be prophetic and can come true later, as has happened often, with a harrowing accuracy, in predicting disasters . He is restless and tired before and during storms. He has many more fears than the "Wood-Man:" fear of illness, the future, spiders, death and the dark. The "Heart-Man" is probably the only type who feels better after consolation when there is heartbreak or other calamity. He easily confides in his friends and talks about his problems. He easily cries while he does so. His tears and just talking about his problems alleviate his tension. Afterwards he feels markedly better. To the contrary of what you might believe, most people deal with grief in a silent way. Most of the prototypes learn to express their grief through therapy but it does not come naturally to most.

Curing Frank was not an easy task. Universal Reactors can't even take regular vitamins, which would be beneficial because, unfortunately, they react to them. Of course, Western medications are out of the question as they either react with a toxic or adverse reaction. But homeopathy has means of treating even the most sensitive patient. I was happier than anyone else to have been able to give Frank back his life.

The Talkative, Jealous "Heart-Man"

I suffer from a disease I don't wish on any of my enemies. I am 40 years-old and can't believe how jealous I am about my wife. We have been married now for 17 years and I am still desperate to control her. It drives me crazy anytime she leaves the house and I don't know where she is going. I become enraged with jealousy if another man exchanges a friendly word with her. It ruins my day. I feel like a fire is burning inside me. It hurts and ruins my relationship with my wife. I am afraid that what I have always feared, a divorce, is inevitable if I don't change.

All this was pronounced in a waterfall of words. His hasty speech was almost an expression of how fast he wanted to get rid of this green-eyed monster. Charles was an intelligent, vivacious, witty person. As are so many "Heart-Men," he was proud and ambitious but clearly suffered from the effects of his frustrations to deal with his situation. As we have seen, a "Wood-Man" deals with frustration by becoming irritable, but the flamboyant "Heart-Man" becomes more boisterous and talkative. He masks his sense of inadequacy and personal hurt by loquacity and arrogance. Charles forgets that loquacity storms the ear but modesty takes the heart. This jealousy is really an expression of self-love from which a "Heart-Man" easily suffers. Of course, a jealous man always finds more than he is looking for. Unconditional love is centrifugal and radiating. Jealousy is selfishness and centripetal, or aimed at ourselves. It can correspond to the out of balance "Heart-Man" who has a tendency to become narcissistic. The whole center of the world revolves around him, not because he is as academic and wise as the "Wood-Man," but because he easily perceives himself as beautiful, elegant and radiant. His anxieties and pent-up emotions find a relief through logorrhea (abundance of words).

Often in the "Heart-Man" two forces are simultaneously at war: love versus hate, arrogance versus humility. Charles was living two lives. One was the proper life of the devoted, loving husband. The other one was a life of deceit, suspicion and insecurity, a life of repression and one which had taken a toll on his physical and mental health. A "Heart-Man" like Charles can become an alcoholic for totally different reasons than the "Wood-Man." While the latter becomes an alcoholic because of his fast life-style, for Charles alcohol is an outlet for his pent-up emotions. His desire for alcohol follows the same course as his emotions: a struggle between keeping it in check and succumbing to it.

It is not easy for any person to confess to being jealous and possessive. Men have even more difficulty with it since they see it more as a situation of competitiveness and amassing power. For these men, there is no jealousy; their behavior is only a positive stimulus for achievement. Charles' jealousy really originated from disappointed love he experienced before he even met his wife. He therefore, was resentful, easily offended, assumed a lot and anticipated before anything really happened. He used vulgar language in his anger, was obsessive and bitter, and easily insulted his best friends. A dose of Ignatia did miracles for this "Heart-Man." It saved his marriage, and no doubt, extended the quality of his own life.

The Wonderful Performer

I hate it when I don't find the energy to do all these wonderful things I have in mind. I am a barber but my greatest love is acting. Every night I go to acting school, play out these wonderful scenes with my friends but the next day I have a hard time, physically and mentally. Lately, I am drenched in sweat at any time, day or night. Sometimes, I have fits of depression, crying spells and fatigue. All these come on with no apparent cause. My clients tell me that they don't know what mood I will be in anymore so they walk on eggs around me. That is not the normal me, Doctor, and I hate being that way.

I had known Sebastian for several years. He was usually cheerful and optimistic, even exuberant. He always talked about the dozens of good friends he had and was always sympathetic and unconditionally supportive towards them. He was a refined looking man, proud, glowing and sparkling; Sebastian was glitter. All these attributes are the reflection of a "Heart-Man" in balance, but therein lies the danger. The "Heart-Man" loves fun, life in the fast lane (not necessarily with work like the "Wood-Man") and lives only for the present (quite the opposite of the hard-working "Water-Man"). Because of his limited staying power, emotionally and physically, the "Heart-Man," who loves to do many things at the same time, literally runs out of gas before he has finished his many projects. He has a sensitive nature and a strong inclination to the arts, which makes him one of the best actors. Sebastian himself was an artist, both in his profession as a barber, where he was known for his original, outrageous coiffures, and in his beloved hobby as an aspiring actor.

> I can't give up this acting, Doctor. That is not a solution for me. I might feel tired, I might feel sick, but when my fellow students applaud me, I feel as if I'm on the top of the world. They love my flair, they tell me I am intelligent so there is no way I could ever give this up. I might as well die. People tell me how good I look for my age (he was 49) and frankly, maybe I can't play the role of a man in his late 20s' anymore , but 30 I definitely can!

This is a normal statement for a "Heart-Man" since he pays much attention to how he looks. He is dressed in the latest fashion, is always well-kept and spends a considerable amount of time before the mirror. At home he is surrounded by mirrors since he loves to have a quick glance at his hair, making sure that it looks alright. Sebastian, while at work, looked in the mirror to check himself out as many times as he checked out his client. For a "Heart-Man" getting older is the worst thing. He will do anything to look younger, including lying about his age and taking a passport photo to a professional to be retouched, making him look younger. He is the last one to tell you that he has grandchildren because it continually reminds him that he is growing older. He wants to stay young at heart, get dressed up and be glamorous. He remains a child at heart, invariably leaves a good impression on other people and is always able to touch their lives. He calls them Darling, Sweetie, Sweetheart, Love, because that is the way he feels. It might lack the sincerity of a "Water-Man," who is deeply attached to his partner, but it comes as naturally to this "Heart-Man" as sunshine after rain.

He is always charming and responsive but what happened to Sebastian often happens to the "Heart-Man:" he is constantly overextending and spreading himself too thin. Inevitably, he crashes because his desire to perform does not match his stamina. He is very intuitive and dislikes academics and serious subjects (contrary to the "Wood-Man"). He loves small talk; the "Heart-Man" considers it bad taste to be wise all the time. To him it is like being at a perpetual funeral. He knows the latest plots of the soap-operas and talk shows and has a powerful romantic streak. Everyone else considers him likable, very engaging and optimistic. Although he does not like excessive mental work, the "Heart-Man's" mind is quick and agile serving him well in one of his hobbies: crosswords puzzles. For a "Heart-Man," the mere act of purchasing books is often mistaken for the assimilation and mastering of their contents. He primarily reads novels but buying more serious books is not part of his repertoire of "must read." However he likes poetry for it heals the wounds inflicted by the world.

The "Heart-Man" brings his enthusiasm and flair to every conversation. He easily exaggerates when he tells you his symptoms. "You have never seen a case like mine, Doctor" is an attention-getter but he smiles while saying it. This is much different from the "Water-Man," who seriously thinks he has the worst possible case in history and even derives satisfaction from it if you confirm it. The difference between the two is also that the intelligent "Heart-Man" often talks with his eyes while the shallow "Water-Man" listens with his ears. The "Fire-Man" is very forgiving and is not ashamed to admit that he has been wrong, which is to say that he is wiser today than he was yesterday.

Sebastian is the true "Heart-Man:" his goal in life is obtaining pleasure, leisure, excitement and a life style without discipline, a true hedonistic personality. Quite the contrary to the "Wood-Man" who pursues pleasure with such breathless haste that he hurries past it. The "Heart-Man" will make it his first and most important goal. The importance of money is second only to glamour. If he has money in his pockets, he will spend it and worry about it tomorrow. "Don't worry about a thing," is his motto. His disdain for the nine-to-five world is accompanied by a penchant for the mysterious and exotic. Traveling to foreign countries, mingling with the local people in their markets and chit-chatting idly over a cup of tea with the Arabic merchants are highlights of his life. If you marry a "Heart-Man," you marry an adventurer!

The Butterfly Lover

I must not be meant to be married. I just
left my third wife and, you would think, I
had learned something. I already am in
love with the pretty girl next door. Everyone tells me I am on the rebound, but
Shelly is so exciting and stimulating. And, I
hate to be alone. I don't think God created
us to be by ourselves, don't you think,
Doctor? I truly believe that Shelly is the one
for me. I feel that I am really in love for the
first time.

Oh, yes. I had heard that before. You wonderful, dreaming poet, Richard. You are the butterfly who smells the flower
for a short time and then leaves it to smell another one. The
"Heart-Man" follows only his heart, never his reason (which
exists in minimum amounts anyway). Every time he falls in
love, it is "the best," "the only love I ever knew," "the real
thing." Infatuation comes easy to him and he perceives far
more qualities in his lover than she possesses. Richard never
seems to have trouble attracting other females in his life.
His charming, romantic nature, combined with his natural
good looks, easily attracts a "new woman" to his life. In his
case, love truly is blind and marriage restores its sight. Hence,
the "Heart-Man" often has a history of multiple marriages
and relationships. Not that he is afraid of committing, like
the "Wood-Man" but he gets bored quickly once he feels
the partner's initial infatuation has waned. He loves the constant adoration and appraisal stowed upon him. He has more
pictures of himself in his house than of his wife and children together. Once the attention of the partner is gone, he
easily gets a crush on someone else, usually much younger

than he is, who would definitely suit him better (his needs, that is). Of course, his love is always a passionate one. He falls in love head over heels and will tell his partner to stay at home and give up her job. The idea that his wife's attention could be turned to someone else is torture. His favorite wife will be the "Earth-Woman" with her docile and admiring nature, pleased with an uneventful life at home and ready to adore her butterfly-man when he returns full of exciting stories. When some younger woman leaves him, he will cry out loud: "My heart, soul and ego are with her. I have had thoughts of suicide, mainly by slitting my wrists." (Notice the dramatic overtone, as an actor reciting Hamlet). Don't believe it. If there is some physical beauty left, this passionate "Heart-Man" will not mutilate himself but rather look for the next flower in the garden who is "lucky to have him."

> I am afraid I am never going to get my life
> together. I am not getting any younger. I
> am starting to lose some of my good looks
> (Oh vanity of the "Heart-Man"!). Time is
> rapidly running out for me, Doctor. What if
> no one ever wants me again? It looks like I
> am using up all my chances. I couldn't
> stand to be alone in my old age.

Richard expressed the biggest fear of the "Heart-Man:" confronting a life by himself and losing his beauty. There is no other prototype who loves company as much as he. Talking to his friends about his problems makes him feel better immediately. Sure, he has been in psychotherapy most of his adult life but where else does he gets so much attention? True to his life style, he hopped from one psychotherapist to another. He would explain this change, "I got bored," which you can translate, "The excitement was gone, the initial interest of the psychotherapist has waned a little." For the "Heart-Man" a long distance relationship never works well. Yes, short absences would quicken his love, as he could get that new burning attention over and over again. But a long absence surely kills any love in his heart. "Out of sight, out of mind" is written for the "Heart-Man" who desperately needs that constant attention.

The love-making of a "Heart-Man" has its own tell-tale signs. Any place for him is a good place to be talkative, even in bed during intercourse. He will speak more and more during the act, overflowing the object of his love with romantic amorous sentences: "You gorgeous looking thing, you make me feel better than anyone else. You princess, you make me feel like I am going to die from joy, etc." He creates a theater setting and makes love with his spirit above anything else. And when he reaches an orgasm, his cry will be heard in the whole neighborhood. Nothing stops him from expressing this highlight with the short fire he experiences. He is the man who will create an ambiance, a psychological atmosphere by talking fantasies, or viewing a film or reading Playboy or watching pornography. Once the act is over and he has gone to the bathroom, he will return to bed and to his partner feeling the "need" to discuss "his life" in an never-ending stream of words. While he is busy talking, he loves to be massaged and rubbed. He is thin-skinned, very ticklish and bruises easily. His favorite erogenic zones are the neck, the feet and, especially, the abdomen below the navel. It is not unusual that the unbalanced "Heart-Man" has a tendency to be an exhibitionist with a desire to expose his body. The ideal place to do this, and where such shameless wildly passionate behavior is tolerated, is the dance floor.

He loves free-style dancing since he really does not want to show off his partner but rather his own body and good looks. The "Heart-Man" loves to live in such a fantasy world. He views himself in this world as very successful (based more on what he should achieve if he is not dreaming his life away) and never has a lack of self-confidence. He is the firecracker that gets the attention but at the end, he rarely fulfills his potential.

A "Heart-Man" often needs another person like an "Earth-Woman" or a "Water-Woman" to ground him. Of course, the "Heart-Man" is usually more attracted to the butterfly, exotic woman. No doubt they would have fun together, but they would soon tire of each other in a couple of months. Before Richard married the new exciting woman in his life, I prescribed for him the right homeopathic remedy. This grounded him so well that his physical stamina improved allowing him to accomplish everything he wanted to do. Furthermore, he was less confused and unsettled without focus. He had become a desirable "Heart-Man," ready to commit to a woman who had more than skin deep beauty.

You have seen some of the light and dark shades of the "Heart-Man." To summarize them emotionally:

The "Fire-Man"

Passionate, superficial, loves change and travel, dreamer, romantic, lives for today, low physical and emotional stamina, sportive, good-natured, playful, attention getter, performer, impressionable, confused, insightful, sensitive, fragile, comical, moral, intuitive, jealous, self-loving, adventurous, unreliable and unstable.

Examples are many of the classic actors in Hollywood film circles: Errol Flynn, Rock Hudson, Rudolph Valentino, Montgomery Cliff, all the "pretty boys" in Hollywood. "Fire-Man" is the group who will become outstanding actors, dancers, singers, stand-up comedians, piano concertists, bartenders, astrologists, designers, architects, artists, musicians, sentimental novel writers, interior decorators, TV-show personalities, poets, dancers, and models.

Men who want to pursue any of the above careers do well to have some of the "Heart-Man" qualities. Most of the above professions rely on beauty, creativity, a flair for dramatics, personality, individuality and short bursts of magnetism and high-strung performance. The "Heart-Men's" profession is not what you can call the run-of-the-mill job from nine-to-five (leave that to the "Water" type). The "Fire-Man" loves the irregular hours, the highs of unusual things to do, interacting with other people, putting his own talents and body in the lime light, and the mystery and untouchability that surrounds his person. Every day is pursued with the highest intensity and passion as the "Fire-Man" realizes that time is his enemy. In almost everything he pursues, and in order to become successful in his profession, he has to have a degree of narcissism, putting himself before everyone including married partners. No wonder that very successful actors sometimes have less success in the marital department. In their pursuit of continuous glory and honor, their partners usually will play second fiddle to the attention they seem to get from the outside world. Since the actor has to prove himself over-and-over again, life evolves completely around his wishes, his projects, his looks, his feelings and his future. There is only room left for an "Earth-Woman", a "Water-Woman" or another successful "Fire-Woman." As long as both "Fire-Partners" are very successful, marriage can be stable and fulfilling since they bask in each other's sunshine. But watch out if one falters. The other partner always moves on: success for only one spells doom for the marriage. This is equally true for two artists living together. It is interesting to watch the presentation of the Oscar Awards and see the actors and actresses arrive for the event. When you look at their faces you know that they have been living for this moment. They pose for the photographers, show their white teeth, wave to the adoring public (who are all aspiring "Fire-People" or "Earth-People"), have outrageous clothing on and soak in the attention of this short glowing moment. But that is what the "Fire-Man" lives for: only the short burst of fluorescent light illuminating his person. Life should be one big party. What glory, what a triumph! He is, unfortunately, the one who becomes depressed and lonely when the light stops shining on him. Only the more balanced "Heart-Actor" seems to age well and pursues roles in every stage of his life.

The Physical Clues of the "Fire-Man"

This man is tall, slender, narrow-chested with delicate features. He is also the young, slender person who grew up too rapidly and therefore has a stooping posture. He has long eyelashes and big-looking blue eyes. His eyes reflect all his emotions with no arrogance or dominance in them but rather a lively curiosity. He stands out through his graceful almost effeminate manners. His skin is pallid, almost transparent, but flushes easily with color when embarrassed or excited. He talks with vivid and rapid movements of the hands as if to fixate the attention on the expressive face.

Often he has a dimple on his chin, always a sign of sympathy, sociability and a desire for company. He is good-natured, sensitive, loves to do good but is also impressionable. His big eyebrows have a round form. These are the eyebrows of the sentimental man, who loves walks in the moonlight, recites poetry and sings tender, romantic songs. Some "Fire-Men" have a "beauty mark" on their cheek. If it is made artificially, it is a sign of coquetry. As a physician or a friend, never forget to compliment the "Heart-Man." Tell him, "You have this magnificent light in your eyes today" or "What a colorful shirt. It suits you really well." After saying this you will see a heavy weight lifting from his shoulders. The world becomes an easier place to live in. Another tell-tale sign of susceptibility and impressionability is the redness or well-colored upper part of the ear. Don't tell this man, "You look like you are dying." You would be thrusting a dagger into his heart! Look at his fingers and nails. You often find oval nails on long slender fingers. It is a sign of a man who likes to dance, who is sensitive to color and beautiful flowers. His fingers are usually longer than his palm and they are full of life; agile and agitated. He can spread-eagle his fingers to accentuate his delicate and elegant hands. His teeth are long and narrow while the gums tend to bleed. Tears come easily to this man, running over his red cheeks in short spastic attacks but can be promptly interrupted by an infectious smile, especially if he is entertained.

Although he dislikes heat, the "Fire-Man" detests the winter months, at which time of the year he becomes a recluse. Not because of the cold temperature, which he likes, but because of the darkness. Being full of light himself, he needs the constant stimulus of growing energy, like Spring, to sustain his bubbling, creative personality. The "Heart-Man" often suffers from Seasonal Affection Disorder (SAD).

It is a time where the otherwise outgoing man likes to go to bed early and get up late and certainly not before it is light. The sun is valued by the "Fire-Man" for its radiant light, putting warmth and life in his heart. Not that his sleep is uninterrupted. Usually he falls asleep easily but wakes up continuously in a sweat, as if his fire has to be put out over and over again. Being a psychogenic sponge, it is hard for the "Heart-Man" to be oblivious about all the good impressions his mind soaked up during the previous day. Be it exciting or unfortunate events, he struggles with equal force to "put water on this fire." Only a controlling "Water-Wife," through her logic and coldness, putting everything in the right perspective, is able to ground an excessive "Fire-Man."

The heart function is to pump the blood everywhere it is needed. An unbalanced "Heart-Man" therefore is easily physically and mentally exhausted, always in need of a nap, which revives him easily. He craves especially bitter things, likes coffee and tea, which always seem to revive him, but are easily abused. He is more indifferent to sugar and salt. When he takes you to dinner, the ambiance of the restaurant has to be at least as important as his choice on the menu. He loves candle light dinners, beautiful napkins, and food that is colorful and beautifully arranged. When he laughs with open mouth, have a peek at his tongue. Either the whole tongue or just the tip of it is red, an expression of the intense short-burning fire within him. His favorite colors are red, crimson, pink, fuschia and orange.

The "Fire-Man" and His Diseases

Most of the diseases afflicting this man are related to the functions of the Heart. In Chinese medicine, the Heart is named the *Emperor*, commanding and controlling all the other organs. It disperses the blood in the vessels everywhere in the body to assure the nutrition in the organism.

This man is the first one to succumb to cardiovascular diseases. Hypertension, angina pectoris, strokes, heart deficiency, arteriosclerosis in general, and infarcts result from his easily aroused emotions coupled to a physical lack of endurance and strength. The Heart commands the speech, so it is no wonder that he is loquacious. However, stammering or stuttering will overcome the unbalanced, shy "Heart-Man."

Insomnia with waking up during the night and hyperfunction of the thyroid are again signs of his easily aroused nature coupled to anxiety. But above all, the "Fire-Man" is susceptible to *mental disease* in all its gradations: from the daily neuroses to the most outspoken psychiatric disease like schizophrenia. When overwhelmed, his unstable character can be transformed by hysteria, anxiety and incoherent speech. He will sigh continuously, feels a sinking feeling in his stomach or a bolus in his throat and experiences a sense of suffocation. His mind is confused, there are feelings of despair and guilt and there is a tendency to have a nervous breakdown. It is as if the solo-performer, always putting a lot of pressure on himself, finally succumbs with a derangement of the mind as a consequence. Sometimes it is a short distance between genius and mental illness. As I mentioned before, the "Heart-Man" can be full of fears, of being alone, of being in the dark, of thunderstorms and lightning, of poverty and of spiders and insects.

In general we can say that the "Fire-Man" is more of a delicate structure than the "Wood-Man," physically and emotionally. A "Fire-Man" always has to pace himself, something which does not come easily to him because of his impulsive nature. He will never take his disease too seriously, asks for quick solutions and is easily impressed with quacks who offer quick cures. It is hard for him to stick to any implemented rules, diet-wise or life-style since his whole existence is based on explosive, short-living joys, no matter what the consequences will be. When he nears death, he always thinks he had a "full life:" he got away with the most toys!

What Made Him a "Fire Man?"

First of all, there are many exterior circumstances that can add a layer of "Fire" to this man. What occurs more often is that the constitutional "Fire-Man" will be most susceptible to these external triggers. Where other people, subjected to the same causalities will have no reaction, the "Fire-Man" will have a reaction to a mere fraction of the same source. What are they?

I will start with the most bizarre, but not uncommon ones. There are several popular books out now that are written by people who got struck by lightning. The event changed them, especially on an emotional basis, which would be the case with anyone who has had a near-death experience. Some, however, receive extraordinary senses from the event, like clairvoyance. Some of the most famous clairvoyants derived their gift after a fall on the head. The Dutch man, Gerald Croiset, is an example. He became famous by resolving some of the biggest mysteries in humankind and was frequently asked to be a consultant by police forces everywhere. More common are out-of-body experiences by patients under anesthesia, even at the dentist. Although it is mostly not a frightening incident, many children don't talk about this experience until later. There is no doubt that all of the above men are "Heart-Men." They are the impressionable ones and they are the ones that will be very sensitive to anesthesia in general. It will take them a much longer time than anticipated to "come back" from their induced sleep. As I have mentioned before, exposure to pesticides, fabrics, electric powerlines, perfumes, paint odors, gasoline, and almost anything in this world, including modern medications, can exaggerate the "Fire-Man" or create a "Fire" layer if the person is subjected to the toxin repetitively.

Life style plays an important role. Smoking, drinking too much coffee and tea, which are craved by the "Heart-Man," and a lack of physical activities easily adds a "deficient Heart-layer" to the person. But none of the above comes near to the most frequent triggering factors: emotions. As the following patient examples show some are more or less obvious.

The Impoverished "Fire-Man"

I am depressed, don't want to get out of bed. When I finally get up, I feel zapped. I have no desire or energy to move, I don't want to see my friends. I get recurrent colds, have swollen glands, can't digest my food anymore and I am pleased if I have a bowel movement every three days. I feel like I have to eat constantly otherwise I get a hypoglycemic attack. Frankly, I should watch my food intake, because I am getting too fat. And lately I have caught myself having one too many alcoholic drinks every night. It's like the air has left me.

Paul looked like he was depressed. He was unshaven, had no life in his eyes and his clothes were wrinkled and unkept. He was a retired bank manager but somehow retired life did not seem to suit him. When he continued talking, the reason became very clear.

> I was really doing well until last year,
> Doctor. I enjoyed myself, played golf daily,
> went out with my girlfriend, could afford a
> good restaurant once in a while, just like I
> always figured it would be when I retired.
> But last year the stock market changed
> everything. I had put all my savings in
> stocks and got wiped out in one day. It was
> a nightmare. I am 67 years-old, and have
> no means to make that kind of money
> again. I should have killed myself like
> some of my friends did.

Paul had gotten a raw deal indeed. If he was a "Wood-Man" he would pick himself up and create new circumstances to restore his savings. But Paul was the typical "Fire-Man" who needs the money to keep a glamorous, exciting life going. That money was the key to fun and therefore the "sunshine" in his life. Take the sunshine away, and life is not worth living anymore. It is interesting to note that Aristotle, a Greek philosopher (°384 BC., †322 BC.) already said that "The heart is the place where the ore of man's knowledge is refined into the gold of his wisdom," connecting the heart and gold. Paul had consulted many doctors and received numerous diagnoses: depression, Chronic Fatigue and Immune Dysfunction Syndrome (CFIDS), hypoglycemia, pre-diabetes, manic-depressive psychosis, spastic colon, fibromyositis, etc. All of this described one or more symptoms of Paul, but none of it covered the essence of the case. He was "Never well since his financial loss," a situation unfortunately more frequent than we might think, especially for the "Fire-Man." He has a tendency to dream up big schemes but unlike the "Wood-Man," who has the drive and stamina to follow up some of them, his energy and interest waxes and wanes. He overextends himself, always dreams "big" and most often of all the prototypes goes into debt and becomes impoverished. He is then an individual who is easily angered, suffers from worry, depression and melancholy. With his flair for dramatics, he often considers committing suicide. The loathing of life and despair may sometimes become obsessional. Not being able to play a round of golf with his friends and buy them a beer is equal to a death sentence for the "Heart-Man," who lives to be surrounded by people.

It is interesting that in his case the homeopathic remedy, Aurum Metallicum or the metal gold, was his solution. "Like Cures Like," the universal law of homeopathy saved Paul from further doom. A financial loss situation was restored by "homeopathic gold," the most desired and most powerful noble metal. These patients often claim, "I have lost the sunshine in my life," (besides money, more frequently, a lifelong partner). We can summarize that a financial loss can lead to an unbalanced "Fire-Man."

The Happiest Man in the World

I can't sleep through one night. I wake up
about every hour after midnight. My mind
is crystal clear; I feel like I drank a whole
pot of coffee. I might as well start my day
at three o'clock in the morning because my
rest has ended anyway. I feel wired. I live
on nervous energy and am afraid that I am
going to crash sooner or later. Doctor,
would a sleeping pill help?

It sure would be an easy way out for Josh but one with
disastrous consequences. Too many patients are already
hooked on barbiturates and anti-anxiety pills. For a homeopathic physician, it is the *suppression* of symptoms, going
against Nature's Laws. The one consequence is always the
same: ever-increasing doses are required to obtain the same
effect. And once addicted, a long painful struggle is required
to get off these drugs.

It's not that I have a problem at home or at
work, Doctor. I have everything going for
myself: a great wife, an exciting job I love
and wonderful vacations. However, it has
been one year since my energy seemed to
be steadily decreasing. Of course this weird
sleeping pattern does not help. I dread
going to bed and postpone it as long as I
can. Nothing seems to help. I have taken
some calming herbs but I might as well be
taking candy.

Apparently Josh was right. There was nothing negative going on in his life. And no Sherlock Holmes doctor had find any clue to his mystery. He had resisted sleeping pills as a solution till now, but he was very tempted at this point to start some. "So what happened one year ago, I asked?" As usual, it was the million-dollar question.

> Well, I got married to my long-time sweet-heart. It was my dream come true. It truly was the happiest day in my life. Just before the wedding I got a promotion at work, so we could afford to buy a new home immediately, adding to our happiness. But strangely enough, it was around that time that my insomnia started. How can that be Doctor? I had nothing but happy events happening to me. I was truly the happiest man in the world.

That statement clinched it for me. There is such a thing, I explained to Josh, as an overload of joy. Five thousand years ago the Chinese had already acknowledged how too much joy affected the heart, leading to insomnia, and in worse cases, even to hysteria. Health is a balance between all emotions, "good and bad." You need fear and worry as much as joy. If you have no fear or worry, you put your own life at danger. But none of these emotions should stand out according to the Chinese wisdom. This is a strange concept to the Western mind who chases a life of joy, thrills and laughter. However, as the history of homeopathy and traditional Chinese medicine show, a person should try to stay even in his temperament in order to avoid disease, especially mental illness. All the happy events, marriage, job promotion and moving into a new house, were too much of a "shock" to the impressionable "Heart-Man" Josh. Can you imagine what happens if you win two million dollars? You probably will not sleep for a couple of nights, thinking about all the things you would like to do with this money. Josh got his "two million" and lost his sleep. He felt like he drank too much coffee. The wonder of homeopathy is that Josh's remedy was Coffea or the homeopathic coffee which restored his restless mind very quickly. I don't have to tell Josh anymore that joy can be a danger if it does not come in teaspoons!

The Heartbroken Youth

I am very concerned about the mental attitude of my son Jeffrey, 17 years-old. It started three months ago when Jeffrey, normally a quiet teen, started to become aggressive. Around that time he was involved in an altercation at his school. Despite the school admitting extreme provocation, he was suspended. He took that suspension very badly and felt betrayed as the school agreed he was not the provocateur. He became very aggressive, especially after being put down by his friends. After this Jeffrey showed the greatest rebellion to authority.

I felt that Maria, his mother, had not told me everything. Sure, there was a change in his behavior. His protest to authority (school and parents) followed an incident in which he felt betrayed. From then on he was easily offended, over-sensitive and ready to explode at the slightest contradiction. But I doubt Maria would have consulted me for a behavior often seen in a teenager. The pathology was much more extreme and became evident as his mother continued in a soft voice.

> It became worse, Doctor. He would go off by himself, come home at all hours of the day or night and would not say where he had been. This was completely foreign to his previous behavior. And then his delusions started. Although he is an average sportsman, he was going to enter all major surfing competitions. One day he was seen in town barefoot in a wetsuit seeking sponsorship. His delusions of grandeur escalated. He was going to be the school athletic championship and play soccer at the highest level. He was going to open a surf shop. He was going to get a sponsor and be set for life. He started eating on his bed and when I told him to go eat in the kitchen, he abused me with foul language. When he had his first attack, he started yelling in fear that he was hearing voices. He hissed saying I was not his mother as he did not live on this planet.

That of course, was not your typical teenage behavior, but deep pathology which Western medicine probably would refer to as schizophrenia. He was put on the usual, heavy medication, and this in spite of the doctors telling his

parents that Jeffrey "was a normal 17 year-old." In Homeopathy these delusions of grandeur, coupled to the statement that he did not belong on this planet, are called, "the
Cleopatra Syndrome." These patients live "as if they do not
belong to their family." They sometimes claim to be of royal
blood and often say that they do not belong to the human
race or to this planet. They have contempt for everyone and
look down on anyone. They have high pride and a high
opinion of themselves with scorn for other people. They feel
that they are rare, noble people and become dictatorial, disappointed and bitter.

This mental illness does not come out of the blue. Where
Western medicine often is satisfied by putting the patient in
a category (schizophrenia in this case), I really wanted to
find out why a normal boy of 17 turned into a major mental
case. Homeopathy tells us that this Cleopatra Syndrome is
caused by grief, rape and disappointment. Obviously, the
incident at school and the handling of it was a disappointment, a betrayal and grief to Jeffrey. I also had no doubt,
that this young man had to be a "Heart-Man" in order to
react so intensely to this incident. The "Wood-Boy " would
have shrugged this incident off and been pleased to be away
from a "boring" place. Clearly, Jeffrey was very sensitive to
criticism and went off the deep end. I wanted to be sure that
there were no other factors. If anything, I wanted to have a
confirmation of other similar incidents. "Were there any
other griefs, any other disappointments, just before his first
attack, " I asked his mother? Maria hesitated for a few seconds and then said in a sad voice:

> Maybe I always have been a little too hard
> on him. He was not doing well at school
> and just before this altercation, I told him

how disappointed I was in him and com-
pared him to his younger brother who is a
very successful student. I have to admit
Doctor, I have been putting him down this
way for quite a while. Naturally, his father
and I are quite proud of our younger son
and it is hard not to bring this up and
compare him to Jeffrey.

Maybe so. But for a "Heart-Teenager," those comments
are like daggers in his heart. He is easily offended and extremely sensitive to criticism to which he can react either in
silent grief or violent fits. To him, it is also a betrayal by
people who are the closest to him. As a result, he lacks self-
confidence and self-respect and starts reacting negatively
to any authority figure. This is really a defense mechanism.
He has felt intense pain (As if someone rubbed salt in an
open wound) and the only way to avoid additional pain is
to withdraw and be hostile when approached. It is as if this
youngster says "You are not going to hurt me anymore, I
refuse to listen to you, I withdraw in my own world, another planet where I am important and stand out." Compare it to the heartbreak in an adult who will say, "I am not
going to get involved in another relationship, nobody will
ever hurt me again."

Jeffrey was a loner, and his parents were very strict with
him. One month after the school incident, he was involved
in a minor car accident on a rainy, slippery night. They
grounded him for two months and made him pay for the
damage. After this, his delusions of grandeur increased dramatically. I have no doubt that these repetitive griefs pushed
him over the hill. This dramatic example shows how important it is for us as parents to understand and know our

children. Early recognition of their son's "Heart" type and by reacting differently, could have avoided some of the damage. In Jeffrey's case it meant more understanding, loving and accepting of what he was (less bright than his brother), rather than inflicting strong criticism on an impressionable boy.

Grief and heartbreak are two factors causing an enormous amount of damage that can lead to any possible disease, mentally and physically. The pathology can be very extreme, as you have seen from the above case. Often I have noted heartbreaks before the onset of many immuno-suppressed conditions like multiple sclerosis, lupus, rheumatoid arthritis and scleroderma. I often think that it is the inability of Western medicine to counteract the tremendous effects of this psychological trauma that lead to the onset of these diseases. For Western medicine, there are no causes known for these illnesses. I have no doubt that grief plays a major role. The two types who are most susceptible to heartbreak in this fashion are the "Fire" and "Water" types. But their reaction is different. "The Heart" type will mainly react with mental illness, ranging from neurosis to hysteria and schizophrenia. The "Water" type becomes a crusader for a cause, isolates himself and grieves in silence. He will react more with physical diseases like bone disease, prostate problems, bladder and kidney disorders. Only a study with many of these victims would confirm these thoughts. I can state this after what I discovered when reading the two hundred year history of homeopathy and its successes and what I have seen in my long-time practice. To anyone, stricken by grief or heartbreak, (and who has not been) I would say, do not underestimate this trauma! Restore it with the right homeopathic remedy (often Ignatia and Natrum muriaticum or sea salt). Remember what I said about rubbing salt in an open wound. When it hurts that much you need sea salt or Nat. mur.!

To summarize:

Causality "Fire-Man"

Heartbreak, financial loss, too many happy events, anesthesia, lightning, pesticides, electric powerlines, grief, disappointment.

Supplements and Homeopathic Remedies to Balance the "Fire-Man"

I have no doubt that there is no other medical modality more successful in treating mental disease than homeopathy. In Western medicine we have a limited potential of drugs available to us and almost all of them have major side-effects besides being suppressive in nature and not covering the onset of the disease. Where medical "mental" drugs only cover a small part of our pharmacopoeia (about ten pages), the topic "Mind" covers the first ninety pages of our Repertory, a book which we consult to find the remedy to cover the exact symptoms.

Ignatia or St. Ignatius' bean and Natrum muriaticum have to be on the top of the list for heartbreak. No other remedies cover this trauma so well. For the deep depression with suicidal tendencies following financial loss or loss of a long-time companion, Aurum metallicum or the metal Gold has often brought miracles. I will not go into further details regarding other grief remedies since it is the job of your homeopathic physician to find the right one tailored to your needs and personality. For anyone suffering from heart disease or hypertension, it is a good idea to *add* to your medications Crataegus *tincture* (Hawthorn berries). It has a tonic effect on the heart muscle. Take 10 drops three times a day in a little water. Incidently, very few doctors realize that the drug digitalis originally comes from homeopathy. According to their own figures, 60,000 patients a year die from the use of digitalis. No one has ever died from the use of homeopathic digitalis (6C). This is only one of the unfortunate examples of turning an effective, safe remedy in a more dangerous drug in name of profit.

Some vitamins are outstanding for the heart function. The king among them has to be *Vitamin E*. Originally discovered by a Berkeley scientist and touted as an aphrodisiac (since rats were reproducing more when fed wheat germ oil) it was called "the shady lady of vitamins." But now this lady turns heads in respectable places. A massive study conducted at Harvard (120,000 people participated) and published in the *New England Journal of Medicine* (May 1993), showed that people who took daily megadoses of E had a 40% lower risk of heart disease and strokes than those taking placebos. It only confirmed what holistic physicians have been prescribing for the last forty years. As a source of nutrition, Vitamin E is not particularly important. Its absence in your diet will not make you sick in the way a shortage of Vitamin C can cause scurvy. But as an antioxidant, Vitamin E is crucial. There is no better fighter against free radicals which we generate as we breath. These unstable molecules roam throughout our bodies bumping into and damaging whatever cells they pass by. These free radicals contribute to a host of illnesses: cancer, heart disease, organ deterioration, arthritis and even the common cold. It looks like life is an incurable disease. But you can knock them out before they knock *you* out. This is where Vitamin E, Vitamin C and beta carotene come in. Take Vitamin E, 400 U.I. daily (usually one tablet). If you want even more benefit from the same amount of Vitamin E, add *Selenium 100mcg* to your vitamin regimen. Another vitamin for good heart muscle function is *Magnesium, 1,000 mgs* daily. To avoid atherosclerosis, fish oils (EPA) have proven to be effective in a Western medical study. These fish oils contain omega-3 fatty acids that have the capacity to lower triglycerides and cholesterol and cause a decrease in the stickiness of platelets. Take two capsules daily. If you are a fish eater, the best rich source of EPA is salmon, herring, trout, mackerel, sardines, tuna, albacore and anchovies. *Gingko Biloba* already mentioned for its antihistamine like action in the "Wood-Man,"has a reducing effect on the stickiness of the blood platelets, often the result of stress, a poor diet or diabetes. It is the better response to the "aspirin" solution since it will not have the risk of excessive bleeding. Other cholesterol decreasing supplements and food substances are alfalfa, ginger, lecithin, onions and garlic. Bon appetit!

If you recognized yourself in the "Fire-Man," make sure to take some of the above supplements. Or even if you are not a "Heart-Man" but you are caught in a "Fire" situation (stress), Vitamin E and family will come to your rescue. If you recognize yourself as this type, then you know to what you have to pay attention. Before calamity strikes (as described in my previous patient cases), take your constitutional homeopathic remedy. Life will be indeed sunshine!

FIVE

The Earth-Spleen Man

The Child: Delayed and Obstinate

> I am worried about Charlie, Doctor. He is 4
> years-old and has had nothing but ear
> infections. He is always on antibiotics and I
> am afraid this is going to hurt him. He is
> also a late bloomer. He only started talking
> when he was two and he still does not talk
> much. He is very withdrawn and seems to
> be happy only when I leave him alone.
> Comparing him with my other kids, he is a
> slow one, nor does he seek out the friend-
> ship of other children. I don't want him to
> be a loner.

While his mother Sophia voiced her concerns, Charlie
stared intently at me. He was just sitting there quietly, looking directly in my eyes. His strong, serious stare reflected
his independence. This was not a shy child who tries to avoid
eye contact, but a child who belied the first impression one
would get by looking at his physique. His head was big,
sitting on a body that I could call fat and flabby. His chubby
face and rosy cheeks made you want to pinch them. Although it was not hot that day, I noticed excessive perspiration on his face. He was slouching in his chair, like he was
not going to move for the rest of the day. Charlie did not
fool me. Behind his flabby body I could sense his strong
character.

> He was not only late in talking, but the soft
> spots on his head (fontanels) were late to
> close. He was late in getting teeth and
> when they came in were poorly formed.
> And he is not like my other children when
> it comes to bowel habits. I am very con-
> cerned when he does not poop for three
> days. When he does go, I can't believe the
> amount that comes out of this little fellow.
> And the smell, Doctor! It smells so strong
> and sour that I always know when he has
> gone to the bathroom.

This poor dentition and the late closing of the fontanels clearly related to a disturbance in the calcium metabolism. "And no," his mother said, "he did not seem to feel uncomfortable when he did not poop for three days. It is almost like he felt more tired after he pooped." While discussing his plight, Charlie had managed to slip to the floor, take his mother's purse and was playing with her credit cards, rearranging them one by one. He seemed to have a good time, minding his own business. There was no doubt about this boy. After all I was told and from what I observed, I knew he was an "Earth-Boy," all right. He was born with an enormous head, had a perspiration soaked pillow by morning, was fat and fleshy with "little bounce to the ounce." He is the typical blond, blue-eyed fat baby over which grandmothers squirm and claim to be so healthy-looking.

He is slow in his development, especially walking, talking and comprehension. The "Earth-Child" discovers early on in life that he is not as quick as his siblings. This is one of the reasons he loves to play by himself. It is a good way to avoid ridicule from his peers. He has the best times when left alone and allowed to proceed independently. But don't interrupt him to do something else before he finishes his project. The "Earth-Child" is concentrating so hard on finishing that any interference is considered a punishment. He will yell and have a temper tantrum which can last much longer than with any other type of child. His comprehension is so slow that it is a long time before he realizes that he will not get what he wants. It is almost as if he does not want to do what you want him to. The reality is that he wants to finish the project he is working on first. Imagine the battles that can ensure between this obstinate child and the controlling parents who are unaware of the typical mental structure of their young boy.

As if the "Earth-Boy" has not struggled enough with his mental slowness (which is not the same as being dumb, just give him time!), physically he seems to be less armed to withstand disease. There is no other prototype (except maybe the "Metal-Lung" boy) who gets more ear infections and colds. Because of the pain and the thick, yellow discharge, he is constantly at the doctor's office where the exasperated physician prescribes antibiotics on a regular basis. He throws his hands up when the mother asks if there is anything that can be done to stop this torrent of ear infections. "Bring him back when he is sick," is the answer. But often, these recurrent attacks can lead to a buildup of mucus in the Eustachian tube, leading to hearing impairment and mouth breathing. One thing parents should not try to suppress is the constantly running nose of the "Earth-Boy." This discharge is "normal" for this child and ensures that a flow of toxins are released from the interior to the exterior. Give unwarranted antibiotics to suppress it and you will often see that this is the beginning of those recurrent earaches. Sore throats develop easily, especially after playing outside in sunny but cold, windy weather. Since he easily overheats, he will take his clothes off and catch a cold the same night or the next day. His constipation, as mentioned by his mother, is very particular to this type. The "Earth-Boy" remains cheerful when constipated and is exhausted after a bowel movement, the contrary of what happens to any other type. The effort of expelling a large amount of feces can be very painful, especially when combined with hemorrhoids or fissures (cuts in rectum). If anything, it leads to even more constipation as the child is afraid to have a bowel movement. Because of strong perspiration especially on the head, in the neck and around the genital area, often a diaper rash and later, yeast rashes, develop with much redness, itching and burning.

You would expect this child with all his layers of fat to be a hot-blooded type. Nothing is less true. He is very chilly and is generally worse in cold and wet weather and very susceptible to catching colds when the weather changes from warm to cold.

> And the nightmares Charlie has! He wakes every night up screaming about monsters and ghosts and nothing consoles him until I get him in my bed. When I would give him a glass of warm milk at night to help him sleep better, he does not seem to digest it very well. He complains about pains in his tummy and cramps, so I stopped doing that, too. He would just cling to me in bed until I finally a put little light up in his room. And what is it always with this boy, Doctor? He constantly asks questions about God and dying. What does it mean to die?

Am I going to die? Where will I go? Are
you going to be with me? and What about
those angels? It does not stop and I can't
brush him off. He wants a logical answer.

Sophia did not know but an "Earth-Boy" often has terrible night terrors. He is very impressionable about what
happens around him. If someone in the family dies or he
sees a violent picture on TV, inevitably it will a subject of his
dreams, causing him to wake up screaming. He is afraid of
the dark (he always needs a night light), of spiders, ghosts,
monsters, and of being alone, especially when he is sick.
Then he wants to be held by his mom, who can't let him go
or he will start crying again. Don't approach him in haste or
with a loud voice or the little fellow will run away and hide
under the skirt of his mother. He has a fascination with the
supernatural, even after growing up. But as a child, he is
impressed with religious teachings, and takes it very seriously when the pastor, with his booming voice, talks about
sinning and going to hell. He will pester you at anytime
with his questions about what happens when he dies or if
God is going to be there for him. It has nothing to do with
future Sainthood but rather it is information that he is not
able to process so he can't let go.

"Let's go home, Mom." Apparently Charlie's limitless
patience had come to an end. In his case, a constitutional
dose of Calcarea carbonicum resolved most of his problems:
no more nightmares, no more perspiration, no more rashes,
no more dizzy spells. No he has not changed into a skinny
kid, yet. Since the first dose 1 ½ years ago he has had no
more ear infections. Repeating the same remedy will keep
him in good health for many more years. There is no doubt
about it. Half of the boys born in the United States will be

"Earth-Boys." I am sure their mothers will recognize them.

The Teenager: Complacent With No Self-confidence

> I am afraid, Doctor, that something is
> wrong with Joseph. He is too quiet, always
> sits by himself at home, playing his com-
> puter games (in which he excels). At school,
> he does not seem to do well. His teacher
> screams at him a lot because he does not
> seem to listen. He does not read well but he
> is good in math. When I try to encourage
> him to get good grades at school, he does
> not seem to be interested or care about that.
> He is not at all like my older son, Lou, who
> is very competitive. I wish I could transfer
> some of his fierceness to Joseph.

Joseph was a "big kid," a teddy bear not a bully. He had a friendly open stare, and was dressed in a simple colored T-shirt and baggy pants. His hair was long and on his face, accentuating big rosy cheeks on a big head. I sensed some awkwardness in this pleasant unassertive boy. I could imagine, that unless he had a good sense of humor, it would be hard for him to survive in a world full of teenagers who love to bully less fortunate boys.

> He is too good, Doctor. Even when his
> friends at school make fun of him, he
> remains calm. They push him around,
> laugh at him, but it looks like he lets it roll

off his back. They call him "butterball" but
he has learned to take the teasing on the
surface.

Not quite. The "Earth-Boy" has the capability to absorb
many things, apparently unharmed. Like most fat boys, Joseph suffered constant humiliation with generally good
cheer. But there is a deep sensitivity to this boy. Often, his
answer to this kind of abuse will be silence. He withdraws,
heart sick, and looks to the company of younger kids whom
he adores. They in turn, love his warmth, his big figure with
assumed power and his generosity. There is not "a mean
bone in his body." He is eager to please and generous to a
fault, a fat kid desperate to win the acceptance and approval
that his thinner peers can afford to take for granted. He is
cautious in choosing his friends, but once you are his friend
you are his friend for life and he will fiercely defend you
against injustice, much more than he would do for himself.
He remains rather a child at heart. It is understandable that
he feels more at ease with smaller children since he is slower,
less articulate and physically weaker than his peers. They
can put him in a closet, they can push him around and often
he will not even react. It is almost that he lacks the ability to
stand up for himself, which is often the case. One of the reasons is that he abhors violence and confrontations, contrary
to the "Wood-Boy" who loves to fight. But watch out when
he finally has had enough. He might lash out with a vigor-
ousness few expect from him. But it takes quite a bit and he
usually shrugs of these incidences as part of his life.

You can compare him to a weak, sensitive creature who
builds a wall around himself for protection. The huge body
often hides a very sensitive heart; bad news on TV or in the
newspapers can affect him dramatically. The plight of home-

less people, of war scenes and violence disturb him tremendously and if anything, isolates him more from his peers who absorb the same information with a degree of indifference or excitement. What can he do for protection? He will withdraw in his own "house," his body. Nobody can be as stubborn as an "Earth-Teenager." He will not give the impression of being hurt, but he will not talk to his tormentor for days. He is not as vindictive as the "Water-Man," who will hold a grudge forever. For all his giving he is fiercely independent as he has experienced that there are few people he can truly trust. Ultimately, the "Earth-Boy" counts only on himself and surrounds himself with dogs, which he really adores. Of course there is something secure in the predictability of the behavior of these animals. The animals' unconditional love matches his generosity. Many unruly, stubborn "Earth-Teenagers" are "suckers" for dogs, and animals in general.

Don't think for a moment he is dumb. He is slow but not dumb. Because he is so logic and down-to-earth, he will come up with solutions of which nobody has thought of. But he does not like the competitive pressure of school or of the world for that matter. The concentration of the "Earth-Boy" is excellent but don't interrupt him. A "Wood-Man" can get up and do something else for ten minutes and then pick right up where he left off. An "Earth-Man" is easily distracted and takes almost any opportunity to escape from chores he does not like (school work). He completely loses his train of thought when interrupted so he needs silence for studying. He knows that when he is interrupted, it will be hard to get started again. He is not gifted with the exceptional memory the "Wood-Fire" boy possesses. In fact, because of distraction and especially slow learning, it might take him twice as long to learn something. He learns word by word but once he has it, it is well retained because of the strong foundation on which it is built. Even the more brilliant "Earth-Teenager" has to put more effort forth than his peers just to keep up with them. This does not help to build his self-confidence. The worst nightmares for him are new tasks, tests, speaking in front of people, mingling and talking to strangers at parties, meeting new people, anything *new and uncharted* brings unhappiness, anxiety and fear of failure to the "Earth-Man." This anticipation anxiety can be a source of continuous torture to the point where he just wants to stay home. At least there everything is predictable and uneventful. But usually he is a jolly, likeable person who really enjoys meeting people. If he has a job delivering newspapers, he will be more diligent and accommodating than anyone else. I would hope that the parents who read this will have a better understanding of their typical "Earth-Child." Give your child space and time and you will not find a more loyal person!

The Adult: Good-Natured, Sensitive and Family Oriented

Living in His Own World

I feel completely overwhelmed by life, Doctor. I can't relate to my friends anymore. I don't know what to do with my life. I feel rejected. I am unable to fit in. I am tired all the time, have concentration problems, an upset stomach, headaches and sore eyes. My biggest frustration is that

> I don't seem to be achieving anything and
> never have any money.

Maurice, 38 years-old, seemed to carry the load of the whole world on his shoulders. He was of stocky build, broad-shouldered, but sat deeply sunken in his chair. He appeared frail and vulnerable. His eyes looked dead, drops of sweat formed on his big forehead and every word he uttered seemed to come after a great effort. He looked like a full-back who could be overrun by a school kid. The fullback was soon replaced by a mourning teddy bear. There were no tears, and his stoic look reflected his lack of confidence and unwillingness to fight. I am not sure he would have gotten up even if an earthquake hit then and there.

> I feel anxious when I want to impress
> people or when I need to perform well at
> work. I start falling apart and often fail at
> things I know well. I crave sweets, particu-
> larly ice-cream and chocolate and although
> I love milk, I have reactions to dairy prod-
> ucts in general. I get bloated and feel tired.
> I generally prefer to deal with problems by
> myself unless I feel that someone particu-
> larly understands me, which is rare.

Apparently Maurice had withdrawn within his own "house." I sensed a lot of grief behind this. Was Maurice hurt so many times in his life that he needed to protect himself with this hard shell, hiding the fragile, insecure creature within? So far, he seemed to match the "Earth-Man" fairly well: withdrawn in his protective house, insecure, sensitive, stubborn, putting on a tough front for the outside world, but lonely and depressed on the inside. I was waiting for some statements that would clarify this morbid situation.

Normally I don't like sympathy from others, Doctor. But my friend who sent me here told me to tell you everything. So I will take a chance. Everything started when I left home after a conflict with my father at the age of 24. That was the straw that broke the camel's back, so to speak. When I think about it, I felt rejected by my father from a very young age on. He was too busy with his own activities and never took any interest in what I was doing. I could never please him. He even sent me to boarding school for discipline. When I started high school I did not fit in. I got bullied and tormented at school and became very shy after being fairly outgoing. I fell completely apart when I did not receive enough points to enroll in a selected course. This was a huge disappointment after lots of work.

Maurice's make-up became very clear to me. No wonder, he had a hard time confiding in anyone. No one in his life, his father especially whose approval he was seeking so intensely, ever had any time to listen. By "taking a chance" now, as he said, he came out of his shell, showing his nakedness and fragility, not sure if he could withstand the outside pressure. That was an "Earth-Man" all right. For him, the house, the family means *everything!* But at a very young age, no family was there for him. His attention seeking was seen as interruptive, undisciplined behavior. "Locked up" in boarding school did nothing but increase his sense of loneliness, isolation and lack of emotional nourishment. It damaged his self-worth and self-confidence enough to become the victim of insensitive, "bullying" teenagers in high school. As we have seen in the "Earth-Teenager," being slower in learning and tormented by peers, he often fails in his academic goals. This is what happened to Maurice. Misunderstood and furthermore unloved by his father, he was set up for the life he was experiencing now.

> After that, things got worse. There was constant physical and mental abuse by my father. I dropped out of college and have felt a loss of direction ever since. I moved away from my father to escape his influence and took up a life of drugs and alcohol. I left my first love and started to abuse my new girlfriend. I felt very guilty. I attempted studying again but I could not get motivated. Again, I felt very lonely. One year ago I was diagnosed with Chronic Fatigue since I had flu like symptoms and felt muscle pains everywhere. I have no exercise tolerance anymore. I can't relate to anyone and I have no real friends. I guess this Chronic Fatigue is here to stay forever.

If you were to look for the "guilty" virus you could say the fatigue is here to stay. But, in my opinion, there was no virus responsible for his illness. The forsaken or abandoned "Earth-Boy" could never escape his loneliness nor did he find any real love in his life to steer him on the right course.

An "Earth-Woman," even a "Fire-Woman," would have been able to give him the love and attention he always craved. But his attempted escape from his father failed to some extent. Even after being away from him, the lack of family cohesiveness pulled him down. An "Earth-Man" without a home is a lost soul. It is his castle when he wants to retreat from the outside pressures. No one has this love for home more than the "Earth-Man." The only way for Maurice to survive was to isolate himself from the rest of the world, a severe form of withdrawing into his own protective shell. Thirty years of futile, exasperating search for "home-love" had gotten him nothing but grief and heartbreak. On the surface he looked shy and calm but to the people who knew him better he was moody, sensitive and highly strung. The "Earth-Man" gets stressed-out very easily and tries to disguise it for short periods to keep up his appearance. But all that takes its toll. His aversion and fear to outside pressure was well demonstrated by his fear of public speaking, even to as little as three people. And his fear of rejection, particularly from females, showed the depth of his lack of self-confidence. The "Earth-Man" loves human relationships above all, he will always be present at reunions with friends, at parties or a bridge game where he enjoys the company of his friends, eating and telling stories. He is a very tolerant and diplomatic individual. His sole ambition is to succeed socially and his usual gentle nature lends great comfort to others without probing deeply into their souls. He is the least jealous of all types, joyous and trustful to a fault. Because of this, he commits judgment errors and is easily duped. Since he is be too optimistic and impulsive he can misjudge the situation and spend too much time and money on failing projects.

I felt sorry for Maurice because he had spent thirty years

trying to find his "niche." If he was given his constitutional remedy at a young age, which was Calcarea carbonicum, I feel a lot of this hardship would have been avoided. But even after thirty years, the same remedy he would have needed as a child had the power of changing Maurice as an adult. Two months later, he told me he enrolled at the University, he had met a girl whom he adored (after subtle probing I found out she was an "Earth-Woman"—Great!) and for the first time he felt he had taken his life in his own hands. I am sure his wife-to-be had a gem in her hands: an "Earth-Man" is very loyal, loving, sometimes boring and housebound. Ladies, if that is what you are looking for, the "Earth-Man" is for you.

My Digestion Kills Me!

Doctor, will you please take my intestines out! If it wasn't for them I would be a perfectly healthy man. But I can't eat with joy, just once, because I get punished every time. No matter what I eat, I get bloated, have to unbuckle my pants and pass so much gas that no one wants to be around me. It takes several hours before I feel good and then it is time to eat again. Food has become my enemy. And I love food!

It sounded like the "Modern-Man" syndrome: living in the fast lane, inhaling junk food, no exercise, lots of coffee and other stimulants to keep up the unforgiving work load of life. But no. This was not Travis, 37 years-old. He was not the hard-living "Wood-Man" we have met before. His rosy cheeks on a bulging body had kindness written all over them. His full smile and hearty laugh, heard as he was describing to me the torment in his life, are not found in the high-strung, nervous whip we encountered before.

It is strange, Doctor, Travis continued, my mother told me that I was a "colicky" baby with stomach problems after I stopped being breast fed. I guess I could not stay away from Mom, he laughed. And at the same time, I started having skin problems. Up until that point, I was a good looking, big healthy baby (I see the grandmothers nodding in approval). My stomach problems change for no apparent reasons but definitely get worse when I over eat, sit down for too long and while I work hard. My skin problems are always more or less apparent. All this has led to weight gain, poor sleeping habits and stress from pain. My stomach always feels tight, stressed and full.

If you want to know what man you have in your life, always ask his mother what he was like as a baby! Travis unknowingly had given me the right clues. In acupuncture, we know that the large intestine and the skin belong to the same group. For Traditional Chinese Medicine and homeopathy alike, the skin has a direct connection with the large intestine. If there is overload of toxins leading to a dysfunction of the large intestine, the body's defense is steering the toxins to the skin, the ideal eliminator. Of course, this elimination process goes in spurts depending on the amount of toxins formed and the strength of the patients Vital Energy to push the "disease process" to the exterior. In other words, the "dirtier" the skin looks, the healthier the interior (or organs) are since the patient's energy succeeds to guide the illness to a safer place: the skin instead of the organs.

Obviously, Travis was born an "Earth-Man" and stayed one. Even as a child, the "Earth" type has a bad assimilation and dysfunctional calcium metabolism. "Earth-Children" will easily have teeth caries and slow dentition. The child can have a strange desire for indigestible foods like raw potatoes, plaster, earth, chalk, which is due to the defective assimilation of lime (Calcium) and manifests the desire of the body for an acquisition of the deficient element. He can either have a desire or repulsion for milk, but his system always has difficulty digesting it, even as an adult. It does not help the "Earth-Man's" digestion when his cravings are pizza, ice-cream and candy. No wonder his stomach never feels totally "right" unless he forces himself to eat smaller and more frequent meals.

> If there is anything that makes me worse, it is very sweet foods, like candy, and very fatty foods. I also noticed that whenever I eat too much citrus fruit, I get a rash for a couple of days and canker sores in my mouth. I would like to know why that happens and I really would like to get rid of it. It is very annoying and painful and it seems directly related to my food intake although no doctor has been able to do something about it.

Acupuncture Laws again have the answer. In Chapter

Two I mentioned the different Laws, *Figure 2*, showing that the Liver (Wood) controls the Spleen (Earth). In Travis' case, the "Earth" element is hereditarily weak so sour foods (citrus) stimulate the Liver, which will overpower the Spleen even more and make it even weaker in energy. The canker sores are an indication of this. The mouth mucosa is nothing but the "interior" skin. Travis' defense mechanism (his Vital Energy) pushes the disease from the organ (stomach/ spleen) to the Exterior or skin (internal). Too many sweets (the sweet taste belongs to the "Earth" or Spleen) again decreases the energy in that organ (creating first hypoglycemia, and in a further stage, diabetes). No wonder they make Travis feel worse since he already has a weak spleen. It did not help his digestive system that he consumed a lot of milk and bread until he was 30 years-old. Of course the motto of an "Earth-Man" is: "Living to eat not eating to live." He wants to finish every meal with something sweet, be it pastry or anything he can get his hands on. He will put sugar in his coffee or tea and yogurt on his strawberries. Other favorite meals are those with rich sauces. Unfortunately for him, he has a vulnerable stomach and large intestines. He only loses his appetite when he is overworked, physically or mentally. His "joie de vivre" attitude reflects the motto of the English sailors of the 17th Century: "Everything I like is illegal, immoral and fattening!"

While Travis' physical complaints were all typically "Earth-related," his emotional make-up, we discover as we get to know this type, was not less typical of the "Earth-Man."

> I am very shy. I don't argue much. When
> confident, I will confront a person, other-
> wise I back down. I weep easily at unusual

moments, especially if I see injustice. I cried
a lot when I was young but was told that
boys are not supposed to cry and to not be
so sensitive. Gradually I wept less but I still
get very sad when I am in the company of
grieving people. I have a poor self-image
and like having a repertoire of familiar
tasks that I am good at doing for support.
But boredom sometimes pushes me to try
things I am not confident about doing.

This is the introvert, quiet and shy "Earth-Man" all right.
Very sensitive to injustice either to himself or others and
rallying to see justice done. Rather than arguing, standing
up for himself and fighting, he retreats within his hard protective shell. People might think unjustly that he is indifferent, arrogant or absentminded. Nothing is further from the
truth. In his usual fashion, the "Earth-Man" avoids exterior
pressure and withdraws to ponder the problem at his own
speed. This walling off means independence in a favorite
light, but, in a less favorite one, it is isolation from people
and loss of social contact. He likes nothing more than leading an uneventful life with a certain routine. He is usually
devoid of initiative and apprehensive about new challenges.
He will always be a slow and very conscientious worker,
rarely disappointing his boss. As in Travis' case, boredom
leads to an expansion of interests but usually at the cost of
increasing stress. So the "Earth-Man" often backs off and
settles into his daily routine.

Travis' case was easy to resolve. Skin and digestive problems were resolved with a Calcarea carbonicum dose (10M),
something he would have benefited from enormously as a
child. Adjusting his diet with adequate supplementation

(further discussed) made his life much more comfortable.

My Mind Wants, But My Body Can't

I am embarrassed to tell you about my
problem, Doctor, but it drives me crazy. I
have a new girlfriend that I care for very
much and I don't want to lose her. The fact
is that I am always exhausted after sex. In
fact I feel so wiped out that I become
hesitant to make love again. But this is the
strange thing. My sex drive is very high, it
is just that my body can't keep up with my
mind.

Charles, 26 years-old, looked at me sheepishly as if he
had an unwarranted complaint. But his huge, soft teddy bear
body exuded confidence and openness. He seemed exhausted just talking to me, sitting in my comfortable chair
as if he was never going to leave it. This is one of the "Earth-
Man's" problems all right. Exercise in all forms (and you
can classify sex as such) does not come easy to him. Compare him to the lifeless oyster surrounded by his hard shell.
Activity of the oyster is reduced to a minimum. It consists
of the slight opening and closing of the shell. For the "Earth-
Man" this symbolizes the restricted amount of contact he
wants to have with the outside world. There are some things
he absolutely abhors: going upstairs, lifting things, in fact
most muscular effort makes him short of breath. His face
and neck drip with perspiration, he pants and his reddish
face makes you fear he is going to collapse anytime. His
only comfortable environment is the swimming pool. Not

to swim laps like the competitive "Wood-Man," that looks like utter nonsense to the "Earth-Man." He loves to float or paddle in the water which is not difficult with his enormous body. Hence his tendency is to be lazy and negligent. His fatigue is even more obvious when his stomach is empty (around 11 a.m. and 6 p.m)., his head feels empty and it is impossible for him to concentrate.

In his love making, the "Earth-Man" loves to touch and explore with his hands and lips: he is the "tactile and oral" lover. Hands and mouth become exploratory antennas for caressing and touching. If he is more the active (Yang) type, he loves touching. The more passive (Yin) ones love to receive the touching. He is timid and prudish. His sexual behavior is devoid of drama and tragic passion. Rather it is sensual and superficial. His favorite position in which he often arrives at an orgasm, is the inverse position: the woman is dominant, on top of him. After the sexual act, which often exhausts him, he cleans up in various ways: brushing his hair, washing his sweaty face, putting on a new T-shirt, after which he returns to bed. He will continue caressing and holding his partner, the tactile need reappears. What will elicit his sex drive is often a long rest and a calm atmosphere. A candle light dinner between him and his wife with soft background music stimulates his desire. The erogenous zones in this partner are the breasts, and the tummy below the navel. This originates from his deep maternal affection and his memory of his mother when a baby. No wonder his sexuality is oral, based on closeness and body contact with a predilection for the breasts. Many of these lovers are found in the Orient, the Middle East and Mediterranean countries where men enjoy the excitement of meals coupled with the visual spectacle of dancing women in different stages of nudity (belly-dancing in which a pronounced belly and breasts are exposed). Beauty and sensuality in their eyes are rounded, fat bellies and large breasts which they love to touch.

If you have an "Earth-Man" on your hands, you know that it is not a matter of mind, but a matter of body unable to keep up with the mind in his love making. He needs patience, rest and the right peaceful atmosphere. He is a reliable partner, the opposite of the erratic butterfly "Fire-Man." His constitutional remedy often makes his sexual life more sexually enduring and enjoyable. As Charles told me months later: "My body is finally more in tune with my mind."

Are you recognizing some of these different shades of the "Earth-Man" in your life? To summarize him emotionally:

The "Earth-Man"

Lazy, stubborn, naive, sensitive to sad events and injustice, poor concentration, home-loving, loyal, loves quietness, averse to external pressure, sensitive to criticism, lack of confidence, down-to-earth, logical, comforting, superficial, procrastinates, not talkative, introvert, passive, phlegmatic, tolerant, complacent, diplomatic, animal lover, disciplined, diligent, fearful, not-competitive or ambitious.

What are the professions geared to the "Earth-Man?" You can find him easily among accountants, geologists, mathematicians, school administrators, oceanographers, farmers, statisticians, economists, dietitians, architects, land surveyors, veterinarians, landscapers and foresters. There is the great love for the home and family, the connectedness with the earth and animals and the desire for an ordinary, uneventful life. He has both feet planted on the ground and a common sense found in people of the earth—farmers. Usually he is well organized and moderately fastidious. All this is reflected in his profession.

As seen in Chapter Two, the "Earth-Man" needs to marry an "Earth-Woman" or a "Fire-Woman" who will get him out of his isolation and bring some excitement in his life. A "Wood-Woman" will most likely dominate him. The first kind of marriage will create the least problems.

The Physical Make-Up of the "Earth-Man"

The "Earth-Man" is usually called the 5 F's: fat, flabby, faint, fears and fair.

A "fleshy" body is the right description. Usually he has a round face and open mouth with thick lips and cheeks. He has a jovial, sympathetic and inviting look. His reddish face (sanguine type) might cause you to confuse him with the "Fire-Man" but with the "Earth-Man" it easily transforms in a pale color upon the slightest effort. His facial expression exudes reassurance and paternal friendliness. Even his hands are fleshy: short, large, thick, with a palm in the form of a square, supporting short fat fingers with nails that are barely growing. His shoulders and hips are broad while a short thick neck holds up the round, dilated face. He tends to grow out rather than upwards. His teeth are square or wider than they are long. Usually his occiput (the back part of the skull) is very pronounced: indicating a love for children. He is not very supple, and rather slow to react but when he does, he can be as powerful as a bull. Sometimes he is the strongly built football player or weight lifter. Usually when he competes in a sport it is to lose some weight which he gains back as soon as he stops exercising. As big as he looks, he will be the first one to faint, when it gets too hot or when blood is drawn from him. He deflates as easily as a big balloon with a little hole in it. In spite of the enormous layers of fat he is very chilly and will go to bed wearing his socks. Perspiration is always abundant and seems to appear for no reason. Even without exercise, his neck, forehead, hair and groin area, seem to perspire incessantly. When he shakes your hand, it feels clammy, cold and limp, not the firm handshake of the "Wood-Man." At night he has the inclination to uncover himself in spite of the sensation of cold legs and his aversion to drafts. The dampness, which makes him tired and sleepy, is his worst climate. The worst place for him to live would be in a hot-damp climate like Florida and the Caribbean. In general his resistance to changes in temperature is very low: his lack of endurance and Vital Energy do not allow him to withstand rough weather, especially dampness coupled with heat or cold.

His appetite, as mentioned, is voracious. He is always snacking and his all-time favorite snack, besides sweets, is boiled eggs. But the "Earth-Man" is not choosy; his alimentary preferences are numerous. He is a glutton at heart with a perpetual appetite for sugar and ice-cream. Don't expect him to go to the "nouvelle cuisine" restaurant where a mini portion of food is served in a beautiful setting. He loves "food-orgies," festivals, banquets, and brunches where a vast array and quantity of food is served. The Germans call this syndrome, "Wein, Weib und Gesang," which translates as "Wine, Women and Singing." It expresses perfectly his idea of fun. Of course, after food intake he is the first to loosen his belt to release the pressure built up in his abdomen. But there are few types who will enjoy dining and eating as much as the "Earth-Man." See the film "Like Water for Chocolate" and you will know what I mean. It is a real orgasm for this man. His indigestion with bloating and gas is expressed on his tongue. The middle of the tongue is covered with a white-yellowish fur. The thicker this fur, the worse his indigestion. His favorite colors are all the shades of the earth: yellow, ochre, umber and sienna.

The "Earth-Man" and His Diseases

Unfortunately, when it comes to health, the "Earth-Man" is among the weakest of mankind. Most of his illnesses stem from his passivity. The tenet of Traditional Chinese Medicine holds that everything is based on the balance between Yin and Yang. The "Earth-Man" is outspoken Yin: passive, inert, immobile, cold, damp, stubborn and fixated. This makes him too easily affected and sensitive to compensate for his lack of ability to meet new challenges. Add to this his innate inability to digest food and his lack of exercise, and you will find he is a prime candidate for a host of diseases. Additionally, his lack of discipline when it comes to food will also cause him trouble.

Many of his diseases will be related to indigestion and maltransportation of food. Gastritis, stomach pain, dyspepsia or indigestion, stomach ulcers, diabetes, hypoglycemia, obesity, gingivitis, hiatal herniae, cellullitis, enteritis, pancreatitis, early morning diarrhea, canker sores, constipation and bloating are inherent to this type.

What might be less known to doctors and patients is that the "Earth-Man" is the first to suffer from a host of immuno-suppressed conditions. Auto-immune disorders such as Crohn's disease, Ulcerative Colitis, Lupus, Scleroderma, as well as CFIDS, yeast overgrowth, parasites and food allergies are encountered more in the "Earth-Man" than in other types. For the Chinese, the Spleen, where white blood cells are produced, is the seat of the immune system. The weakness of an "Earth-Man" easily translates into one of these illnesses.

Other disturbances often encountered in this type have been well known in Chinese medicine for 5,000 years. Bleeding disorders, (hereditary such as ITP (Ideopathic Trombocytopenic Purpura and hemophilia) and bleeding gums and nose bleeds are a reflection of the "Earth-Man" in distress who lost the ability to keep the blood in his vessels, or who presents fragile structures without the surrounding defensive wall (the oyster in the shell!). His limp weak nature is also reflected in the prolapse of organs so often encountered in this type: stomach, rectum, bladder, etc.

The "Earth-Man" has many fears: of the unknown, of the future, of poverty, of the dark and of being alone, that he will be ridiculed for his ignorance and fear of losing his mind.

In general we can say that the "Earth-Man," more than any other type, has to pay attention to his health. Sometimes congenitally weak, fueled by a sedentary life style and rich food intake, he needs more than anyone else to discover his constitutional remedy. A regular intake of supplements is needed to support his weak metabolism and lack of grit.

How Did He Become an "Earth-Man?"

A great percentage of the children in the United States are born "Earth-Types." It is only later, around puberty, that at least half of them change into "Fire-Wood" types. But besides the overwhelming constitutional "Earth-Man," certain events, especially emotional, transform that person into the one we have gotten to know. Some examples of my clinical experiences demonstrate this.

The Rock of Gibraltar Crumbles Down

> I am at the end of my rope, Doctor. Any activity whatsoever, any work or stress, any excitement or agitation drives me up the wall. I really feel that I am walking a tight rope and anything extra in my life will make me fall off of it. As soon as I get up in the morning, I feel unbalanced, my legs tremble, and my whole inner body shakes. I feel like I did not sleep at all and I have the greatest difficulty forcing myself to go to work. The longer I lie in my bed, the weaker I feel. I am totally exhausted. I take a short walk and then want to lie down again. My body screams, "Help!"

Andre, 46 years-old, looked much older than his age. His haggard face was full of wrinkles as if he was carrying the weight of the whole world on his shoulders. His graying hair was thinning on the top. He moved slowly around because of a stiff back. He had exhaustion written all over his body. He looked restless, anxious and depressed.

> I am not myself, Doctor. I have become a different person. Everyone knows me as always being ready to help, gentle to my children and wife, pleasant at work and ready to sing a song in the morning. But

lately I am in a mood that makes me feel
like a totally different person. I am indifferent to my wife and children. When my
children ask me something I brush them off
in an abrupt manner. I have violent fits of
anger when my children put on some
music. At work I am now known as an "old
grumpy man" who is best left alone. My
friends don't even phone me anymore.
They tell me I am impossible company. I
am usually generous, altruistic, amiable
and intelligent. Now I am mean, egotistical
and prejudiced. I have become an argu-
mentative, obstinate and narrow-minded
freak. Sometimes I wish I could die; I am so
tired and exhausted. And I hate those
family gatherings around the holidays.

I think the psychologist Jung would have a ball with this
man. "This man," he would say, "is seized by a strong emotion and therefore possessed by a devilish spirit." Clearly,
Andre was not at his best. When this happens, there is a less
commendable part of Andre that surfaces, something Jung
called the *shadow* of the person. Apparently the dark side of
Andre was destroying all his relationships and even worse,
it was killing any feeling Andre had for any living being
around him. He caught himself kicking his favorite dog and
screaming at his children when they asked him to play some
tennis with him. "You go to Doctor Luc," his wife, Ann said,
"or there will be a divorce. I can't live with you anymore."
Put to such an ultimatum, Andre grudgingly made the appointment, wondering to himself what difference a doctor
could made in his exhaustive state. I gently led him through

the onset of this period.

> I think, Doctor, it all started last year. I got a
> promotion at work, but all it brought was
> many more responsibilities and longer
> hours. At the same time we moved into a
> new house which was a fixer-upper. Every
> free moment I had I spent in restoring the
> kitchen, wallpapering the bedrooms, fixing
> the roof. And then Steven, my oldest son,
> got in trouble with the law. With some
> friends he stole some items from the school
> cafeteria. All this was very hard on my
> wife, Ann. She went into a depression for
> three months, during which time I played
> nurse, mother and father. But I kept on
> pushing my body. What other choice did I
> have? Now that most of these problems are
> solved, I feel even worst. How is that
> possible? I always prided myself on being
> able to handle many things at the same
> time, but I must be getting too old for all
> this.

Andre was the typical "Rock of Gibraltar" to which the whole family world would turn. But his responsibilities had increased in dramatic proportions. Being an "Earth-Man," Andre had stoically taken on all these new tasks. Family and duty were not idle words in his mind but his body had limitations. Burning the candle on both ends, he performed as long as the stress was there. He fell apart as soon as life started to look up again. Of course this is nothing new. Many people perform well under stress when the adrenaline is flowing. Caught in an ever-increasing demanding life, they push the limit of their tolerance a little further. This "stretching" can only go so far. Andre had reached his breaking point. He became hysterical, irritable, indifferent, fault finding, intolerant to opposition, easily offended, never happy unless annoying his family members and full of fears and anxieties. This Rock of Gibraltar was constantly worrying about the present and the past. He could not put those unhappy months behind him. "What if this happens again? I feel I can't handle any more stress. I am afraid we are going to the poor house. I can't believe my son did this to me." He could not let go, dwelling on the past to such an extent that it paralyzed his present life. His wife, Ann, could not come near him. He was averse to her company and to any attempts at consolation. His motto was now, "I don't care," quite strange for a man who was known previously as a model of responsibility. Andre was "dead" emotionally, aloof and detached. He simply lost the strength to think or act and was overwhelmed by his work and responsibilities. Called upon to endure the trials of domestic life, Andre had succumbed to their magnitude.

> It is not enough that my mind is playing
> tricks on me, but my body is falling apart,
> too. I feel that my stomach is falling down
> in my body, and I can't digest anything
> anymore. When I sit on the toilet I feel like
> there is a heavy ball in my rectum. When I
> finally go, it is painful because of hemor-
> rhoids and I have this heavy feeling deep in
> my abdomen when I bear down. It feels
> like all my intestines are going to fall out.

As much strength and tone as his mind lost, Andre's body was not far behind. Exhaustive Vital Energy leads to a loss of tone in different organs. The "Earth-Man" who loses his grit is like a structure lacking sand, a piston with no rod. His organs prolapsed, stretching his stomach, rectum, bladder, etc. Gravity becomes stronger than the energy of the Spleen, which holds these organs in perfect tone, and the patient has the sensation of his organs falling out. The "Earth-Man," especially because of his sense of duty and great love towards the family, is the first prototype to burn out; much quicker than the "Wood-Man" who has a much stronger stamina, much faster than the "Fire-Man," who does not have that sense of responsibility and diverts the heaviness of the situation to pleasure, fun and superficiality. The "Earth-Man's" Vital Energy gets overwhelmed and brings him to the brink of depression.

As complicated as this case might look, a homeopathic physician easily grasps the essence of the case. A dose of Sepia 1M brought Andre out of the abyss of despair. He became the joyful, fatherly figure he always had been before.

The Homesick "Earth-Boy"

I suffer from unbearable fatigue, Doctor. If I don't take a nap in the afternoons, I soon feel very tired and get a headache with nausea and sometimes vomiting. I was diagnosed with Chronic Fatigue last year, but the doctor and I have been unable to pinpoint a reason for all this. I am only 23 years-old and I should be in better condition. My doctor found yeast and parasites in my intestines but medications have been of no help.

At first, indeed, there was no special indication why Barry would have become sick with a disease that seems to have become rampant in this century. He did not look particularly sick and his blood tests were all negative except for some viruses found in his blood and the above mentioned yeast and parasites. But why should a young man lose his physical and mental strength? If yeast and parasites were the cause, why didn't his condition improve after drug treatment? I was sure that these micro-organisms were consequences, not causes, of his conditions. The golden advice: go to the beginning of the disease. I asked him to tell me about his relatively short life.

> I was the third of four children. In kindergarten I felt like an outsider, on the fringe, regarding friendships. I was rather shy and unassertive. I remember crying for hours after my mother dropped me off at school. My father was very strict and was particularly hard on me. I was the first boy and he expected great things from me. He pushed me hard. My mother was always kind and stood up for me. I became an excellent student, my father saw to it, and in high school I won a prize for excellence. As a result I was selected to participate in an exchange program to Switzerland for four years. I did not want to go, but my father insisted on it. I did not want to disappoint him since, for once, he seemed to be proud

of me. But those four years were terrible. I
was terribly lonely, could not make friends
and the discipline in the new school was
very harsh. I missed my two sisters and
mother enormously. Looking back, I don't
know how I finished all this. Everything
seems to be in a haze. I hardly remember
anything about those years. I seemed to
have repressed all memory of that time.

It was obvious that Barry was a sensitive child, unac-
customed to being isolated from his family. There was little
he wanted to say about his stay in Switzerland. He was not
like the "Fire-Man" who would have welcomed this adventure or the "Wood-Man" whose curiosity and learning drive
would have taken over this nostalgia for home. For Barry it
was sheer hell and punishment. He had not become a "Man"
like his father had predicted and hoped. If anything, the separation from his family had added to his awkwardness with
other people. His symptoms started soon after his return to
the United States.

I had always been a good student until
then. But upon my return, I experienced a
loss of memory. It was hard for me to
associate two ideas or to find the appropriate word in a conversation. I felt spaced-out
and exhausted. I was drowsy during the
day and couldn't fall asleep at night. I
suffered from headaches with heaviness on
the top of the head. Whenever I tried to
study, I got a feeling of confusion. I lost all
my interests and could not get the strength

together to think. I still feel emotionally flat
now. Not much has changed since then and
all this happened five years ago.

It might be hard for Barry to see what a hardship these
four years had been since he was repressing the memory as
much as he could. It might also be much easier for doctors
to blame yeast and parasites for his demise, but I was not
fooled. The stay in Switzerland was a grief period for him
that literally drained him of the little energy he had when
he left. Devoid of the emotional support from his mother
and sisters, Barry became despondent and lonely. His intense cravings for carbonated drinks and his chronic, pain-
less diarrhea clinched the remedy. A dose of Phosphoric
acidum cleared much of his symptoms. Later tests for yeast
and parasites proved to be negative in spite of no further
specific drug therapy for this condition. But correcting his
initial trauma, homesickness, allowed his Vital Energy to
fight the surplus of these micro-organisms and normalize
their numbers. For me it was another good example, that in
the fight to regain health, the physician should pay more
attention to the person himself rather than to invisible mi-
crobes roaming through his system. And yes, his diagnosis
was "Never well since home sickness," an increasing causality of disease in a time when families fall apart, where
young men increasingly have to suppress their feelings or
anima and are forced to show toughness when confronted
with grief. If you have an "Earth-Child" in your family, be
aware of his sensitivity and his love for the home. You will
save his health!

Causality of the "Earth-Man"

Grief, worry for the present and the past, overwork, too much or too early responsibility, overlifting, homesickness, too much sugar intake.

Supplements and Homeopathic Remedies to Balance the "Earth-Man"

More than any other type, the "Earth-Man" will need additional support from homeopathic remedies and supplements.

The king among the homeopathic remedies for this man will definitely be Calcarea carbonicum as a constitutional for many children and adults. Other possible remedies are Calcarea phosphoricum, Silica, Sepia, Carbo vegetalis, Phosphoricum acidum, etc. Your homeopathic physician will determine the right one for you. Again this can not be the job of the reader. Each remedy covers the "totality" of the patient: physical, mental and emotional. Some of the above remedies have been discussed while presenting clinical cases. It is not in the realm of this work to elaborate about them. But you can expect miracles from the right choice of homeopathic remedy. It will be well worth all your time and effort to find a qualified homeopathic physician.

Supplements are numerous for this type, depending on his weakness. Because of poor calcium assimilation, a combination of calcium and magnesium is necessary (ratio of 2 Mg/1Ca, or take about 2,000 mg Mg versus 1,000 mg Ca). Digestive enzymes are often a big help for the "Earth-Man": bromelain or pineapple enzyme, take 1 tablet after each meal; Polyzym O21, made in Germany but available in the United

States, are rather expensive but superior to any other enzyme; some patients need more HCL or Hydrochloric Acid, to be taken before meals. To cut sweet cravings, GTF chromium, 1 tablet before each meal is a must. It stabilizes the insulin release and therefore curbs the appetite for chocolate and sweets. It is a must for any diabetes sufferer: together with intake of his medications, he will be able to stabilize his condition easier. Other "ant-sweet cravers" are Green magma and homeopathic remedies such as Argentum nitricum.

The memory of the "Earth-Man" is not as good as the "Wood-Man" or "Fire-Man." Take Choline which can penetrate through the blood-brain barrier and is believed to go directly to cells associated with the memory. Usually you can find it under this name in your health food store or it will be under the name of Lecithin which contains choline. Take 2 tablets daily of about 500 mg each. Natural sources of choline in food are fish, egg yolks, green leafy vegetables, liver and wheat germ.

As we have seen, the "Earth-Man" needs to strengthen his immune system more than anyone else. Some of the more effective supplements are the anti-oxidants, fighters of free radicals roaming through your system and injuring cells. Vitamin C is the king. It improves the mobility of white blood cells and stimulates T and B cells, as well as the giant "cell eaters" (macro phages that gobble up and destroy bacteria, viruses, fungi and other disease-causing organisms). It will play a role in wound healing and be very effective in controlling gum bleeding. Take Vitamin C, at least 4,000 mg daily. Be selective about the kind of Vitamin C you take. As always the absorption degree, or how much you are able to get to your cells, is essential. Some Vitamin C is based on a different process (micro dialysis). The unique advantage of the micro-dialysis process is that the rate of drug release is little affected by variations in gastrointestinal pH or enzyme content. "Peaks and valleys" of drug release cannot occur. This effective method permits a continuous rate of release. (To obtain this Vitamin C and all other supplements in this book, see TAD Corporation[†]). Other important anti-oxidants are Vitamin E (take 400 I.U. daily), Zinc (take 50 mg daily), beta carotene (take 25,000 I.U. daily). It might sound like a lot but it isn't. It usually means taking one capsule of each. For this purpose avoid the multivitamins; they don't contain enough of each individual vitamin to be helpful.

Because of his diet, life style and lack of natural defense, one of the "Earth-Man's" biggest enemies is Candida albicans, or the infamous yeast cell so prevalent in the modern population. The newest and best protection for Candida sufferers is homeopathic Aqua Flora™. For anyone suffering from this condition, I advise reading my book, "Candida, the Causes, the Symptoms, the Cure." It is essential and helpful for this type's digestion and liver function to take an acidophilus product (a capsule between meals, keep the product refrigerated!). If your child is under seven years-old, he does not need acidophilus but Bifido bacteria (1 tsp. daily of the powder, refrigerated, between meals will do).

If you have an "Earth-Man" at your side, whether child, husband, lover or friend, surprise him with the present of health, and advise him on how to strengthen his innately weak physical and emotional structures. You will make a gem out of him!

[†]See addendum for information about TAD Corporation.

Six

The Metal-Lung Man

The Child: Frail and Restless

> The fall is coming and it will be the same misery with Ronny as it is every year. From fall till spring, he has nothing but colds, a stuffy nose and sore throat. He has no stamina to overcome these diseases so he suffers relapses all the time. And when he is sick, I have a hard time being around him. He becomes destructive, is irritable especially in the morning when I wake him up. I never know if he is going to hit me or embrace me. I can't go through another winter like that, Doctor. You need to help me with this kid.

Martha, Ronny's mother, looked exhausted and exasperated. Ronny was hiding behind his mother but when she pushed him forward, he reluctantly said hello. He was a scrappy kid with a pale face, almost white which accentuated his "allergic shiners." He looked almost emaciated and anorexic but his sparkling eyes reflected the inner strength of this child. I would not be surprised if he could turn this sparkle into a beam of aggression when needed. His mother could not agree more.

> Sometimes I don't recognize my own child anymore. One moment he is affectionate

and sweet, the next moment he throws
temper tantrums, uses foul language and
breaks everything he can get in his hands.
He never seems to know what he wants. As
soon as he gets his way, he desires something else. You know, doctor, I could live
with his colds if you could fix his mischie-
vous, stubborn character. He is smart:
when he does something wrong, he blames
the dog.

I knew this little 6 year-old Ronny was shrewd enough
to realize that if he was not caught red-handed, he could
not be guilty. His strong character was quite a contrast with
his physical fragility. A "Metal-Child" seems to catch everything that is going around. His weak areas are the throat,
the lungs, the large intestine and the skin. Tonsillitis with
swollen glands, frequent bouts with bronchitis, even pneumonia with high fever, asthma, and all kinds of skin infections, especially eczema and roundworm seem to attack this
child relentlessly. The Fall especially, with its cold-damp climate, seems to shock his finely tuned immune system. But
even exposure to cold wind will wake up his allergies with
a stuffy nose, alternating with production of thick yellow
and green mucus. When TB was at an all-time high in the
beginning of this century, the "Metal-Child" was the one
most predisposed. With the resurgence of TB resistant antibiotics, this prototype could be the most vulnerable. Common childhood diseases such as measles and whooping
cough are always present in a more severe form in this child.
And if you have a child with constitutional eczema, you can
be sure he is a "Metal-Man."

This type of child may need to be obstinate and defensive emotionally just to survive physically. The "Earth-Boy's" fragility has more to do with a defective calcium metabolism and flabby muscle structure, in other words, bad foundation. In the "Metal-Boy" something goes wrong with the defense posts of his body. He seems to get sick from the moment Fall starts till the moment Spring begins. The nose and lung are the entrances of "evil:" allergies, micro-organisms seem to invade effortless into the deeper organs. If he is strong in Vital Energy, he will present mainly skin rashes. The weaker one will suffer from colds, bronchitis and constipation which is present from his first days on. Just like the "Earth-Boy" he can be intolerant to milk, but the "Metal-Boy" never will feel comfortable with his constipation. Not infrequently it can provoke an asthma attack. The "Metal-Boy" is usually thin, pale, with blue eyes, and has a delicate profile with soft skin. People who remember seeing TB children know that this is often their physical description.

Inevitably, the many illnesses from which he suffers does not make him a stellar at school. The "Metal-Child" is usually very reasonable and rather wise, but slow and easily distracted. No wonder he has mediocre school grades from the very first year. Contrary to the "Earth-Boy" he has a good memory with a good analytical mind which helps him to excel later in life in professions unlikely for this type, like a judge. And misery of misery, since life is not hard enough for him already, he wets his bed more often than any other type of child. Once he has turned off his physical and emotional restlessness, he sleeps so deeply that he will urinate in bed. The temper tantrum of this "Metal-Boy" is usually a violent picture: screaming, kicking, throwing himself on the ground. The tantrum is not finished until he gets his way. It is a different picture than that of the "Earth-Boy" whose temper tantrum will be translated in obstinacy or in the "Fire-

Boy" who gives up quickly when he sees that a positive result is not forthcoming. He has the tantrums of the "terrible twos" for just about any reason and once he can speak, he is not shy about using foul language. Just like the "Wood-Boy," the "Metal-Boy" is more capable of violence than are the other types. His capriciousness and unpredictable behavior can easily throw a family in turmoil.

Martha got her wish. As if a miracle had occurred, a dose of Tuberculinum stopped the avalanche of colds and flus. But even more importantly, Ronny's outbursts were a thing of the past. He became more cooperative, gentle and was pleased when receiving rewards without always desiring something else. His pale face color disappeared and the afternoon fevers and night sweats did not return. This case showed the depth of action of the homeopathic remedy, changing the physical and psychological behavior in a very short time span. I knew that it had saved little Ronny from a lot of trouble at school and at home. Instead of becoming a teenager with disturbed behavior, Ronny applied his humor, cleverness and tenacity to become a leader in class as well as on the sports field.

The Adolescent: Insecure, Withdrawn, and Hungry for new Stimuli

When the "Metal-Boy" grows up uncorrected, it is not only his physical health that is at stake. Insecurity, alienation from his peers and general sadness drive this youngster to roam around by himself, uncertain of what he wants in life. His schoolwork suffers, his relationship with his parents can be volatile and physical illness seems to crop up in direct relationship to the intensity of his disturbed emotions. The following case seen in my clinic exemplifies this.

> Steven has problems concentrating on his
> studies, Doctor. He has difficulties sitting
> still, and seems to be dreaming his time
> away. He complains of recurrent headaches
> but I don't know if this is for real or just an
> excuse. He tells me he just does not like to
> study anymore. And he used to be such a
> good student. Now he even has failing
> grades. And it all started after coming
> down with bronchitis last fall. His father
> who is short-tempered and hard-working
> (no doubt a liver type!) has lost his patience
> with him. They fight constantly but the
> only result is that Steven has run away
> from home on different occasions.

Diane, his mother, sighed and waited anxiously for my answer. Steven, 15 years-old, was the prototype of the "Metal-Teenager:" lanky, pale, with an expression of sadness on his face, quite the opposite of the fiery, whip-like "Wood-Teenager" we got to know in a previous chapter. He admitted to me he had changed considerably since he was sick last fall. He simply could not concentrate on long books or study intensively but preferred small articles on varying topics. He hated to sit still for any length of time and told me that despite constantly changing his fields of interest, he could not stick to any of them, therefore enduring the wrath of his father who called him a procrastinator and lazy freak. It is not easy to live with an unbalanced "Metal-Man." He is constantly dissatisfied with everything he does and any event in life. Hobbies and interests are of short duration, and there seems to be no love of life, so necessary to the vigorous execution of any undertaking. To him, life is one long process of getting tired. Very often a disease linked to the lung or skin is the onset of his frail imbalance, as was in this case. But there was more to his health as Diane explained.

> He always was a sickly child, Doctor. When he was born he suffered from eczema over most of his body. The doctors prescribed cortisone creams which cleared up his skin but since then, he has suffered from asthma attacks. I guess living with innumerable asthma incidents has not been easy for Steven. It seems to have taken the wind out of his sails and since then, his whole behavior changed. He became emotionally agitated and always bounced from one place to another even as a baby. I am afraid that his teachers are right when they label him as an attention-deficit disorder (ADD) child. I wonder if those drugs would help him.

I could see where Steven's story started: in the womb. His mother had indeed taken hormones and medications during the pregnancy. This often leads to eczema of the newborn as was the case with Steven. From that point on, Western medicine often makes numerous mistakes. The eczema of the child is really a sign that his body is trying to get rid of the inherited "toxins" (from the medications) by pushing them to a safe place, the skin. The concerned mother and the eager, non-thinking doctor applied cortisone cream, and the disease is pushed back inside the body towards the organs. We call it *suppression* in homeopathy. That this often leads to asthma is understandable when we have some knowledge of acupuncture. The skin and the lungs *both* belong to the Metal group. This intimate relationship is evident in the alternation of asthma and eczema which we often see in practice and is often due to the incomprehensible act of the doctor, applying cortisone creams. I shudder at the fact that this "poison" is available over-the-counter. It surely had affected Steve's life who really never had a chance to become a balanced child. Very often, this dissatisfaction, inattention and restlessness leads to the *misdiagnosis* of ADD (Attention Deficit Disorder): thousands of these children are on Ritalin or related drugs, unjustified!

I asked to be alone with Steven and tried to get to know him a little better. I was not disappointed. Steven's sadness was clarified some more as he softly spoke about his last year.

> I don't like my father. But I could tolerate
> him by escaping to my girlfriend's house. I
> was deeply in love with her. Don't laugh
> but I could not eat or sleep for several days
> when I met her. But she left me after two
> months. I think it was because I am always
> sick and don't have the energy to do those
> things that my friends do. I am easily
> fatigued and my friends laugh at me when
> I want to go home to rest.

The "Metal-Teenager" is a romantic at heart. He yearns for intimate relationships and falls in love easily, but to a much deeper degree than the "Wood- or Heart-Boy." When he is in love, he tends to forego everything, even essentials like food and sleep. When the relationship ends, he often goes into a deep despair and is unable to pick himself up like the "Wood-Boy," who will secure another friendship without holding grudges towards the old love, or like the "Heart-Boy" who might cry as much but not as long, as he is easily distracted by new and exciting people he meets in his life. The "Metal-Boy" is mortally wounded and depressed from thwarted love. As restless as he is, he really longs for security and structure in his life. When it is not there, he wanders aimlessly around, hoping and believing, like a pure romantic, that happiness may be just around the corner.

I believe that the "Metal-Teenager" together with the "Water-Teenager," have the most difficulties during their puberty years. Not being understood, sad and romantic in nature, the turmoil caused by the combination of transforming into manhood and an inept constitution, is often sufficient to bring solitude in his life. He is more likely than any other teenager to be a runaway, looking for understanding and love, and to resolve the intense dissatisfaction ruling his life. Because he often has a negative personality, he creates stress for himself and others. He can be filled with anger and bitterness and focussing these emotions on others, especially his parents. This buildup of hostility prevents the "Metal-Teenager" from having a good relationship with others. He tends to be self-centered, which he views as a defense mechanism to survive this dark cruel world. He has difficulty trusting and feels little empathy or understanding for other people, mainly because no one else seem to understand *him*. All this does not create a strong self image: low self confidence and a sense of low self-worth are often present.

Steven's homeopathic therapy consisted of recreating his early life. Through different remedies, layer-by-layer would be peeled off, much as a psychotherapist would do. When he broke out with eczema, his asthma dramatically improved, proving that the disease was finally going from the inside to the outside and taking the pressure off of the internal organs. Since the eczema was an "old" symptom coming back, I knew Steven was healing because his recovery process was following the Laws of homeopathy. The appropriate homeopathic remedies strengthened Steven's emotional and physical make-up before all his negative feelings became a vicious circle, detrimental to his health.

The Adult: the Personification of Atlas, Carrying the Globe on His Shoulders

The Dutiful, Conscientious Family Man

I suffer from asthma, Doctor. It is strange
how it started two years ago. At that point
in my life, I was shattered to hear that my
mother was diagnosed with cancer. Three
months later I had bronchial pneumonia,
which then evolved in asthma attacks. My
mother suffered for a long time before
dying. This was very devastating to me and
I really don't think I ever got over it. During this time, my asthma got steadily
worse. After my mother's death, my father
came to live with us. One year later, I found
him dead in his chair watching TV. He had
suffered a heart attack. I found it very hard
to come to terms with his death. Since then,

> I have been hospitalized several times with
> severe asthma.

Dick, 44 years-old, looked very much as if his mind was maintaining iron control over his emotions. His pale face did not betray much emotion, a contradiction with the intense grief he was telling me about. His decrease of Vital Energy after hearing the "bad news" about his mother's illness led first to pneumonia and unrestored, to asthma afterwards. "Curing" the pneumonia with Western healing methods does not always result in a restoration of the Vital Qi, as was evident in this case. The "Metal-Man," as personified by Dick, is very conscientious, very family oriented and has an extreme sense of duty. It was only normal to Dick to care for both of his parents, even to the detriment of his own health. The "Metal-Man" is a man of his word with strong principles. He is dogmatic to the degree of inflexibility and rigidity. Even in the face of intense grief, he remains stoic and uncomplaining, always doing his duty by the "book." He is very task oriented with a mind that is systematic, proper and routine-oriented. It is black or white for him, clear-cut and practical. He is correct, stable, very reliable and works hard to support his family who is the center of his attention. This was clarified even more as Dick continued his story.

> My life started to get worse. My wife and I
> had a very traumatic time when my son
> was also diagnosed with asthma. He was
> very ill and had to be hospitalized on many
> occasions. We were advised to move to a
> better climate, which we did, as we were
> very concerned about our son. It did

improve his asthma, but my situation remained unchanged. I am very disappointed about that as I hoped for some improvement for myself, too.

Following his strong sense of duty, Dick had relocated his family which was very hard on him. Apparently the change of climate was enough for his son's Vital Energy to overcome his asthma. But for Dick, moving brought more responsibility and worries since he had to look for a new job, a haunting thought for someone whose illness was limiting his work options. No wonder he was not getting any better.

I also suffer from psoriasis and arthritis. In fact, when my asthma subsides, the joint pains and skin problems seem to flare up. I frequently have a very husky voice and am sensitive to weather changes. I wake up unrefreshed especially after an asthma attack in the middle of the night. Any attack forces me to sit up straight, with my elbows on my knees. I don't burden my family with my problems. I am comfortable dealing with problems by myself and I do not weep easily.

A "Metal-Man" like Dick may appear to others to be devoid of emotions but nothing is further from the truth. He prefers silent grief, not showing his emotional sensitiveness. Typically for this type of man, the mental suppression is so severe that the symptoms of his disease become channeled with devastating force on the physical level. Psoriasis, an angry-looking common skin condition and arthritis, a deformative bone disease, are often found in the "Metal-Man" as the iron-clad mental control seems to have a distorting effect on the body structures. It is easily understood why his asthma attacks occur mainly between 2 and 5 a.m. In acupuncture, we know that each organ has two hours of great energy, which correspond also to the greatest sensitivity of that organ. For the lung, it is between 3 and 5 a.m. Also, since the night time and the sleeping process is a time when the mental control mechanism has the least force, the symptomatic physical expressions become intensified, hence asthma attacks. It translates merely into an unwillingness to let go of his mental control. During the day, his strong emotional control allows him to control the physical imbalance of his body, but at night, this security system operates at half-strength.

The "Metal-Man" is admired by others for his dignity and self-control in the face of difficulties. He has little pretension and a straightforward style of no-apology honesty. Flattery with its intoxicating perfume will conquer the "Heart-Person" but will have no effect on the "Metal-Man." Of course, this intense emotional control will be very difficult on a less understanding wife who will complain about her husband's aloofness and cold-heartedness. Often though, her husband will suffer silently and internally, dwelling over his wife's fortune, looking desperately for a solution to alleviate her distress. This may lead to trouble if a very strong "Metal-Man" marries a weaker "Heart-Woman," which is a relationship according to the Destruction cycle (see Chapter One.) The attention seeking "Heart-Woman" will absolutely not get what she wants, overtly expressed sympathy with her situation. The highly emotional "Heart-Woman" wants to hear her husband express his sympathy and unbridled devotion on a daily basis. If she does not get it, she will move away from this "cold fish" to look for other relationships which, hopefully, will provide the much needed comfort and attention. Her playful and artistic traits have to be acknowledged, something that does not come easy to the "Metal-Man." But if both partners are in balance according to the Control cycle, happiness is bound to happen. The flirtatious, happy-go-lucky "Heart-Woman" will brighten up the life of her sober, dignified husband providing him with some very needed lightness in his life. On the other hand, the "Metal-Man" is a grounding force for the ever-moving and dancing "Heart-Woman," providing her with some healing stability and security.

It speaks for the strength of homeopathy that a patient like Dick can be healed entirely by homeopathic remedies, in his case only *ONE* remedy. In Western medicine, the above patient will consult a dermatologist for his psoriasis, a psychiatrist for his "strange, unloving " behavior leading to family tensions and a rheumatologist for the arthritis. Each of these doctors will act *independently* of each other as if they are treating three different people. What a pity for the patient who undergoes unnecessary treatments, what a pity for the physician who treats only parts of the patient and therefore never will see or be part of the total healing process of that patient. Dick's asthma and joint problems were cured with the homeopathic remedy Kali Carbonicum. Dick was able to express himself much more freely, which enabled his increased Vital Energy to externalize his physical symptoms and ultimately chase them out of the body, which constitutes a true cure. This balanced "Metal-Man" soon became the pride of his family, and above all, the homeopathic remedy had stopped the mental and physical decline of this "rough diamond."

The Pessimistic and Anxious Hypochondriac

> My wife told me that I had to come here. It
> was either this or a divorce. She tells me I
> am always on edge, easily annoyed and
> indifferent to everybody. But you know,
> Doctor, I am very anxious about my health.
> In fact, I feel I suffer from an incurable
> disease no physician has been able to
> uncover yet. I really think I will die soon
> since I don't think anyone will be able to
> help me.

Freud would have had a field day with this patient.
Paul's face was a mixture of anxiety and anger. He did not
like being pushed into this consultation, which in his opinion, "was not going to help him anyway." This is another
side of the "Metal-Man." His seriousness and dogmatism,
if unbalanced, can go too far and with time, the negative
side might start to appear. He becomes discontented and
dissatisfied, stubborn and hard to communicate with. This
patient, who at one point tended to ignore his problems,
giving no symptoms at all to his inquiring physician has
changed into the opposite. He exhibits severe anxiety about
his health to the degree of hypochondriasis, speaks only
about his ailments and never stops asking questions. He will
acknowledge his controlled emotions by describing varying symptoms in his body. His solar plexus is a rich source
of symptoms, most characteristically he feels a "state of anxiety in the stomach," as if his biggest fear is located in the
gastric area. Another expression of his suppressed anger is
diarrhea, especially after taking antibiotics, fissures (rup-
tures) in the skin, especially the anal area and bleeding warts.

> My wife reproaches me for being very
> irritable and she can't put up with my fears
> anymore. But you know, Doctor, she lives
> as if there is only today (here comes the
> "Heart-Wife"), is an uncontrollable spend-
> thrift and does not want to hear anything
> else about my concerns. But I know I am
> right so all we do is fight about these
> issues. Of course, I sometimes use abusive
> language, wouldn't you in this situation?

Paul had put his finger right on the problem. The greatest fear of the "Metal-Man" is his fear of the future, rather
than fear of the present or past like the "Earth-Man." The
fear and worry express themselves in different ways. He
worries about his financial future which instills a fear of
poverty and about his health because nobody will want to
take care of him (a prophecy that often comes true because
of his difficult behavior.) Although he will not freely admit
it, he is extremely afraid of the dark, most likely because he
has an inability to cope with uncertainty or loss of control
over his emotions. Therefore he fears impending disease,
especially cancer, but not like the "Water-Man" who is truly
afraid of catching a disease and sees "polluting germs" everywhere. The "Metal-Man" knows that disease is something
which he cannot control himself and that bothers him more
than the disease itself. He will talk endlessly about his "diseases" draining the energy from anyone who is listening.
And he does not hold doctors in high esteem. In fact, he
continuously blames them for his suffering and holds
grudges against any physician who has not "helped" him.
Of course nobody can help him anyway. Unbalanced, he is
truly the personification of the three "P's:" pessimistic, a pest

and pissed." While to the outside world he will look like a distinguished gentleman always in control of himself; at home he can be a terror. But as Nietsche said: "It is easier to cope with a bad conscience than with a bad reputation" and his reputation is intact. As with Paul, he has this sense of correctness that if challenged, meets with foul and abusive language. If by any chance the other party is wrong and apologizes, he will be unmoved by it since he never forgives and forgets. He has a definite idea of what is "right" and his inflexible mind will not deviate from it. He is the pessimist who ends up by desiring the things he fears in order to prove that he is right.

Mentally, the "Metal-Man" is the biggest pessimist of all the prototypes with a fearful eye towards the future. His melancholy corresponds to the season of Metal: the Fall. It's the season where everything in nature becomes dry, and all the leaves die. There is also the saying, "He is in the Fall of his life." It symbolizes the ripe age of life, reflection and re-gret about things that happened. But rarely will you see se-vere mental disease in him as is the case in the "Heart-Man" with his fragility and susceptibility. Before he loses control over his emotions, he will succumb to deep pathology of one of his organs, often the lung or the intestines.

I prescribed the homeopathic remedy Nitric Acid for Paul. I did not expect him to come back to tell me he was better as this goes against the spirit of the unbalanced "Metal-Man." Even if he is 75% better, he will tell you, "he is no better." But when I met his wife two months later, she thanked me profusely for the great improvement she saw. Paul was not behaving anymore like a two-edged sword with sarcastic and cutting language. In fact, he dared to spend some money on a trip his wife had long dreamed of and stated that it was more interesting than he thought, a high compliment from the previous scruffy polar bear.

The Loyal and Frustrated Lover

I am embarrassed to tell you, Doctor. My wife who is very beautiful and vivacious, loves the attention of other men. She flirts all the time. She tells me it is harmless and does not mean anything. I try to stay calm but somehow it must get to me. I am eating much more than before, have gained a lot of weight and am concerned about my heart. I have already had two heart attacks and am afraid this weight gain is going to cause me to have another.

As usual, the "Metal-Man," John in this case, tries to keep his dignity and integrity in the face of the most heart wrenching difficulties. Married to a "Heart-Woman" who is out of balance, he silently tolerates her insensitive behavior. But his frustration is compensated for by an excessive appetite. John takes vengeance by eating even more, something his wife does not appreciate. The "Metal-Man," fiercely loyal and faithful to his partner, is totally devoted to his relationship. He is a lost romantic with a tendency to sadness and melancholy, silently suffering with secret tears. Often his outlet is to write sad poems about love or to keep an intimate diary in which he can express his deepest feelings that his iron control does not allow him to vent. Psychologically and emotionally, in acupuncture, the lungs are considered to be the seat of our ability to express sadness. If the lungs become weak as is the case with John, there is usually a tendency to self-pity, to be anti-social, and to harbor a somewhat quiet or inward depression, lacking will and vitality. Being married to an extroverted "Heart-Woman," you could see why they would clash.

The "Metal-Man" loves odors during sexual intercourse. Not only perfumes which can be a very erogenous signal to this type, but especially odors linked to the sexual act itself. Curiously enough, but understandable according to the tenet of acupuncture, the Yin-Yang unity, this man either looks for women wearing heavy perfumes or the perfume can be a sexually repulsive factor. Both situations are possible. Like the "Earth-Man" he loves to touch and foreplay will consist mainly of long caresses. He looks for round, opulent women, his favorites. His sexuality is often linked to good meals and alcohol, so he often has sex after meals or a siesta. His favorite erogenous tactile zones are particularly the area below the navel, and to a lesser degree, the thighs, mouth and breasts. After the sexual act, the "Metal-Man" will most likely look for silence and serenity or he will go straight to the kitchen because he is hungry.

Knowing the sexual make-up of the "Metal-Man," it is not difficult to see why John had problems with his wife. His sense of righteousness clashed with the playfulness of his partner. Both needed an appropriate homeopathic remedy which restored much of their happiness. As stated before, a balanced "Heart-Woman" and a "Metal-Man" can have a very satisfying relationship.

You have met the "Metal- Lung-Men" in various degrees. To summarize them emotionally:

The "Metal-Man"

Conscientious, dogmatic, rigid, controlled emotional, apathetic, introvert, meticulous, loyal, family oriented, great sense of duty, stable, reliable, righteous, correct, hard worker, absent-minded, hypersensitive, sad, fearful and worried about the future, anti-social, fear for the dark, romantic, melancholic, ignores his own health problems.

A classical example of the "Metal-Man" is Judge Lance Ito, who presided over the O.J. Simpson murder trial. He controlled his emotions amidst the cacophony in his courtroom. He was conscientious, righteous, meticulous, stable, reliable and hard working. In such a volatile and passionate court case, one could not have wished for a better judge, a fact the defense and the prosecution both acknowledged. And as we have predicted for the "Metal-Man," his proper, dogmatic, "by the book" behavior was quite a contrast to the flamboyant "Liver-Wood" defense attorneys. But just as in the Control cycle, it was the steady "Metal" Judge Ito who controlled the "Liver" defense attorneys.

While the "Metal-Man" will be an excellent judge, other excellent professions in this group are historians, professional soldiers, managers, airline pilots, travel agents, prosecutors, watch makers, police officers, translators and poets. All of these people are very task-oriented. They are hard workers, pragmatic, able people and builders of the society. They are not workaholics like the "Wood-Liver-Men" but they work hard and steady without overdoing it. They are bound by a sense of duty and follow rules more carefully than other people. They have love for order, discipline and the law. The poet is an exception among this group. But he will write beautiful words that come from a suffering, melancholic and romantic heart. No one other than the "Metal-

Man" can write from the deepest abyss of his soul , the only way he has of expressing his longing for love. The other poet, the "Heart-Man," has many more ways of expressing himself; he is loquacious, loves to dance, to flirt, and will take any opportunity and form of communication to share his happiness with others.

As a race the Asian people are the outspoken prototype "Metal." To ascertain a person's true nature, observe how he behaves in adverse and difficult situations. Take the recent earthquake drama in Kobe, Japan (February 1995.) In spite of considerable hardships of food and water shortages, as well as homelessness, the Japanese people remained stoic. Looting was a rarity (which can't be said about similar circumstances in the United States). In spite of a slow response from the government, people were mostly appreciative for what was done or considered it simply their duty to do whatever they could do for themselves. No extreme bitterness, no swearing, but acceptance of their fate and, at the same time, a strong will to rebuild. Emotions were controlled and energy was channeled into practical dogmatic solutions. There is no better example of the balanced "Metal-Man."

The Physical Clues of the "Metal-Man"

The "Metal-Man" is longitudinal bordering on skinniness. He carries narrow shoulders on a weak structure with a spine that has a tendency to kyphosis (slightly convex). Just like his emotions, all his physical movements are also controlled. He is a slow eater, walks slowly and speaks in a deliberate, hesitant manner, often thinking long before answering. He habitually sighs during his speech as if he suffers from grief. This symptom is also seen in the "Water-Man."

Strangely enough, this "Metal-Man" can be one of two extremes: either he has incredible elasticity or he is rigid. The "elastic" man is usually longitudinal, with a delicate profile, white face, soft skin and blue eyes which either are dreaming and evading the world or looking at you in a "steel-blue" manner, sharp and icy. He is the man who has "ice in his veins." The more rigid type expresses his motto, "Law is law" in all his physical traits. His eyes are metallic, hard and suggest no forgiving. A long nose and thin lips stand out in the tortured face which often reflects a calculated mind. His eyes rest on you as if he is sizing you up with an air of mistrust. Or, they clearly express annoyance and a sadness that never seems to go away. His eyebrows are often in the form of the French accent "circumflex," expressing his critical behavior. His hands are long with a narrow palm. He cannot spread his fingers easily but he is able to luxate them backwards effortlessly. Often his vulnerability to cold is expressed in blue-white fingers and in a tendency to wear hats. This is the man who has an abundance of *body* hair but not necessarily head hair.

The "Metal-Man," consuming most of his energy to maintain proper behavior and suppress his emotions, is easily physically fatigued and will often require periods of rest and vacations. Although this seems to be the case with the "Heart-Man" there is quite a difference. The latter loses his energy by expressing his feelings *too much* and jumping from one task to another. But he recuperates quickly after *short* naps which completely revive him. The "Metal-Man" is more careful with spending his energy, likes to go to bed early and get up early.

He loves the "nouvelle cuisine" with its small portions since it suits his small appetite. He loves milk, butter, cheese, chocolate and especially pungent dishes. He also prefers sweets over salty things.

He fears dryness as well as the dampness since Fall seems to be the starting point for a lot of his illnesses. Dampness causes colds and flus which don't seem to go away till Spring comes, while the dryness causes constipation.

His favorite color is white. His tongue is usually pale and narrow, reflecting sharp, critical and deliberate speech.

The "Metal-Man" and His Diseases

The organs belonging to the "Metal-Type" in acupuncture are the lung and the large intestine. Obviously then, these are the weak organs of the "Metal-Man." There is no other prototype that is more susceptible to colds and flus. The slightest draft will cause sinusitis (the nose is the "door" to the lungs), bronchitis, pneumonia from the Fall till Spring.

The more severe lung diseases, asthma and TB, are often transferred hereditarily. TB, which is rising in incidence and becoming increasingly resistant to the present day antibiotics, was appropriately called in the past, "the disease of the sad passions." A typical asthma attack will be between 2 and 5 a.m., with the patient having to sit up to be able to breathe, his elbows resting on his knees. He fears the cold since it attacks his lungs very quickly and he usually feels very chilly.

The other weak point is his digestive system, more precisely the intestines. Because of his inherent sensitivity (to noise, touch, any insignificant emotional trauma is a major event), he is prone to the Western catch-all disease, "Irritable Bowel Syndrome." This consists of cramping, diarrhea, bloating and gas but his physician finds nothing specific on his X-rays. Very often the diarrhea drives him out of bed early in the morning, between 5 and 7 a.m., the hours of the large intestine in Chinese medicine. This chronic early morning diarrhea is the unpleasant wake-up call of the "Metal-Man." Because of irregular bowel movements, hemorrhoids are a common trait.

In Chinese medicine, the skin also belongs to the element "Metal." While he is suppressing his emotions and therefore driving the disease inwards on a physical level, good Vital Energy is necessary to push this disease process outward. No other prototype will suffer more skin pathology. Eczema, rashes, psoriasis, mycotic or yeast diseases are just some of the more common ones.

While mental disease is rather rare in this type, his extraordinary worry about the future can lead to depression. He can drive any optimist crazy with his stories of gloom and doom which in his opinion, has to happen. Stoicism here has become extreme and in order to avoid grief, the "Metal-Man" prepares and expects the worst. If unbalanced, he can become the eternal pessimist making him fit company only for an identical twin. He has an outspoken fear of darkness and easily suffers from anxiety with a feeling of "fear in the pit of the stomach."

A typical "Metal" endocrine disorder is the low thyroid function (hypothyroidy) which explains his chilliness, and his slowness in his actions and words.

In general, we can state that the rigid mental control of the "Metal-Man" can be his strength as well as his weakness. His strength will protect him in less favorable situations to remain stoic and practical; his weakness will translate in a crumbling down of his body structure with arthritis, skin diseases and a fragility of the pulmonary system.

How Did He Become a "Metal-Man?"

What are the different conditions which make a person a "Metal" type and therefore predisposes him to the illnesses mentioned before?

The "What If" "Lung-Man"

> Doctor, I hardly made it to your office. I had to stop three times to go to the toilet. Each time, I have loose stools and, frankly, I need to use your bathroom even now.

While Frank did just that, I wondered where this intensive action of intestines came from. Parasites? Infection? Ulceration? Or simply "nerves?" Frank filled me in.

> You know Doctor, it all started when I was preparing for my promotion examinations. I studied long hours, was often very fatigued, and I increasingly lost some self confidence. I continuously asked myself, "What if I fail? What will people say? And what if I succeed and I get sick from over studying so everything I am doing now is in vain?" As I continued studying, Doctor, I always found another "What if" which surely would sabotage my ambition. And strangely Doctor, my diarrhea started around the same time. Now I can't go to a store without having to know where the restrooms are.

Frank exemplifies well what happens if worry (of future events) takes over someone's life. He suffers from anticipation anxiety: he anticipates so many problems that he will never find the strength and courage to execute his plans. He always finds a "What if" so strong that it will have physical repercussions, especially diarrhea and stomach discomfort. This can become so extreme that the person in question does not dare leave his home. They dread going to a public place, the theater or public gatherings for fear of having diarrhea. It leads to irrational, impulsive behavior with a morbid dwelling over the future (just the contrary of the "Earth-Man" who will dwell over the *past*).

Worriers about the future are constantly excited and hasty. They are driven and do everything fast. Time always passes too slowly and in order to calm their nerves, they have rituals and superstitious behavior. They tremble easily, especially when confronted with new events. Their deepest fear is that of losing control (which they literally do when they lose stool in their pants). This fear of impending doom leads to tormenting thoughts: "I am not going to succeed," " I am a failure and no-good," "I might as well be dead, I have no purpose." There are many conditions in which worry of the future is predominant but some stand out even in normal circumstances as part of the daily life. Actors and actresses have a constant battle with stage fright and auditions. Everything in their future is depending on a successful next audition, and even landing a role in one film does not provide them with any security in the future. Often actors and actresses, who are mainly "Heart-People," transform into "Metal-People" when success is not forthcoming. In a different but similar setting, students at any level, but especially at the college level, are confronted with anticipation anxiety about examinations. As was the case with Frank, cerebral tiredness from over studying led to the evolution of a "Metal" situation or layer. It is the "Metal-Man" who will always be very nervous before the event, leading to a further weakening of his constitution if he remains unbalanced. Besides "emotional" diarrhea, he can suffer from stomach ulcers, esophagus ulcers and in extreme cases, from colitis.

Frank's situation was resolved with a dose of Argentum Nitricum. Any student suffering from anxiety before examinations could very well benefit from this remedy. Frank promised that if he had to study intensively again, he would come to me before calamity happened. Kali Phos is an excellent "student" remedy for cerebral fatigue consequential to overwork and for loss of memory.

The Overstressed, Grieving Teenager

> Doctor, I recently started a new job which I like very much, but I am afraid I may be sacked because of the amount of sick days I have to take. My worst problem is nausea which occurs suddenly without warning. It is mostly unstoppable and when I start vomiting I am unable to keep working or go to work. Lately, I have had also recurrent respiratory infections. They have become more frequent, last longer, are more "aggressive" and I have to take time off work. I am not just getting any better.

Of course, David, 22 years-old now, had been to many doctors before consulting me. He was diagnosed with gastroenteritis but the regular medications were of no help. He told me it all started prior to his last semester of college. During that vacation, he was working in a supermarket and at a printing shop. Apparently this stressful situation was not the only thing that happened in his life.

> Around the same time, my best friend's father committed suicide and his three year relationship with his girlfriend ended the day before the funeral. My friend became emotionally very reliant on me and I felt under a lot of pressure to help him. Shortly after this, my sister married. Early in the marriage, her husband began physically, verbally and emotionally abusing her. I felt extremely helpless and enraged at the same time. It is extremely difficult to discuss this abuse with anyone, even with my girl-friend and my own family. It took several months before I confided in my girlfriend.

It looked to me that several factors were causing David's illness. First, there was the situation of overextending him-self in work. What was worse, being very sensitive and jus-tice oriented as a good "Metal-Man," he felt enraged and helpless knowing the extent of abuse his sister was endur-ing. This was a heavy burden on him. He felt the grief and indignation of his sister and worried about what the future held. His sister was still married to the abusive person and therefore it remained a continual worry. And it looked to me that he was carrying some his best friend's grief on his own shoulders. I had almost decided on my prescription for a homeopathic remedy, when I asked him if he ever had these attacks of nausea and vomiting before (since this was his foremost complaint).

> This nausea has occurred twice before in my life. The first time was when I was 11 years-old. I went to a new school to attend a special class for intellectually gifted students. I stayed there for 5 months, getting good grades but was extremely stressed by the pace of learning. I had a bizarre experience in which I was looking at myself, as though I was outside my body. I was screaming and sobbing hysterically, unable to stop. This "breakdown" got my parent's attention and they quickly transferred me back to my old school. But I have never felt well since then. Four years later I had a second episode of fever, nausea, vomiting, diarrhea and pain in my abdomen. After blood tests, X-rays and an ultrasound, which were all negative, the General Practitioner told my mother that "It's all in his head. He is just stressed." At the time I felt very depressed, hopeless, afraid of nuclear war and death.

It is interesting that David went through two causal factors of a "Metal-Man:" overstudy and worry about the future. As intelligent as he was, the new school stressed him to his limit. He felt obligated to stay there to fulfill his parent's high expectations, but he felt exhausted, lonely and not accepted by his peers. But as his body was communicating to him in his "delusion" or "vision" how much pain and grief was present, his doctor quickly dismissed him as a "psychosomatic" because all tests results were normal. The second episode reflected the introvert character of David. He suppressed his emotions about his fear of the future, the nuclear war he envisioned and the fear of death. Don't forget, he was an impressionable 15 year-old kid at the time. He really represented the emotional controlled "Metal-Man."

> I like to share my problems with someone I feel I can trust but I find it difficult to trust someone enough to really tell them my inner feelings. There are still many issues I haven't gotten the courage to discuss with someone. On the whole I tend to be a very private person. It is usually a "last resort" action for me to talk about my problems with another person, and then only when I am absolutely sure I will benefit from their input.

David's rigid control over his feelings channeled this negative impact on the physical level with devastating force: nausea and vomiting were just one response of his body. His further decline of Vital Energy resulted in frequent respiratory infections. I am happy to say, the homeopathic remedies Nux Vomica and Tuberculinum saved his health and his job. Even more, David did not remain the same worry wart or the overachiever everybody else wanted him to be.

Causality of the "Metal-Man"

Continued worry about the future, grief, smoking, environmental toxic factors, too many pungent foods, too many sweets, cerebral fatigue consequential to overwork.

Supplements and Homeopathic Remedies for the "Metal-Man"

It is obvious that the weak point of the "Metal-Man" is his lungs. Therefore attention needs to be paid to this organ first. Different homeopathic remedies able to strengthen the constitution of the "Metal-Man" have already been discussed. Tuberculinum, Kali Carbonicum, Bryonia, Argentum Nitricum are just a few mentioned in the clinical examples. Many more are available and your homeopathic physician will be able to determine the one that best fits you.

Supplements are important for this man. First is Vitamin C again, and in particular, the Vitamin C with microdialysis diffusion of TAD corporation. Take two capsules daily. Other supplements for colds, flus, sore throats and sinusitis are garlic capsules, twice a day, Zinc 50 mgs daily, Vitamin E, 400U.I. daily, combined with Selenium 100 mcg daily, and Coenzyme Q10. Coenzyme Q10 is a powerful antioxidant that appears to preserve human tissue and restore function following periods of oxygen deprivation. In tests on animals and humans, it has been observed to stimulate the immune system, help control infection, lower high blood pressure, and help ischemic heart disease. It works synergistically with other antioxidants—such as Vitamin E. Take 30 to 60 mgs of Coenzyme Q10 daily.

There is also Propolis, called nature's antibiotic. The concentration of flavonoids is responsible for the major antibiotic effects of propolis. Flavonoids have far-reaching actions, not only against bacteria, but also in treating ulcers, rheumatoid arthritis, influenza, colds, radiation damage and enteritis. Propolis is a material gathered by bees from the leaf buds and bark of trees, especially poplars. They use it as a sealer for holes and also take advantage of its hygienic qualities by building it up as a barrier just behind the hive entrance. These two services—as building material and antibacterial agent—are married nicely in the word "Propolis" which comes from the Greek words meaning "defense before the town." Take 500 mg every 3 hours.

Another useful herb is slippery elm (a tree found in the Eastern parts of Canada and the United States). We use its inner bark in making lozenges for treating sore throats and coughs. It has a gentle and nutritive action.

Echinacea is more than just a pretty flower. The Purple Coneflowers were used by the prairie Indians for more ailments than any other plant. Echinacea roots were used for everything from colds to sore throats, tonsillitis, influenza, mouth ulcers, spider and snake bites. It has been widely hailed in Germany as boosting the immune system in general. Rather than the tincture (use this only in acute situations), take a couple of capsules daily.

For the skin rashes so common to the "Metal-Man," Beta-carotene 25,000 U.I., Evening primrose oil, 3 capsules a day, Garlic, 3 capsules daily, and GLA capsules, 3 a day. Avoid any local application of creams (especially cortisone) for danger of driving the disease inwards and causing severe organic disease.

For gastrointestinal disorders such as parasites, candida, irritable bowel syndrome, colitis, ulcerative colitis, Crohn's disease, etc. use Aqua Flora™, lactobacilli capsules or powder (3 a day between meals, keep refrigerated) for adults and children 7 years and older. For younger children use Bifido bacteria powder, 1/2 tsp. daily between meals. For parasites, use Paratox®, 3 capsules daily and Garlic, 3 capsules daily. For further information about the treatment of these conditions, read my book, *"Candida, the Causes, the Symptoms, the Therapy."*

SEVEN

The Water-Kidney Man

The Child: Introvert, Serious and Fastidious

> I am very concerned about Frederick, Doctor. He is 7 years-old now and hardly has any friends. He is always withdrawn, does not talk much and always seems to be daydreaming. He is almost too serious and not playful like my other children. He is a loner, always has his nose in books. He refuses to go to birthday parties or participate in games with other children. I am afraid he is becoming an anti-social child, shunning everyone, including us, his parents and his brothers. When I ask him "What is wrong?" he shrugs his shoulders and hardly looks me in the eye. Do you think I need to go to a child psychologist? Even his teacher in school has commented on his quietness.

You know when a teacher comments on quietness in class, it must be serious. Peace and calm in the classroom is a desired objective for any teacher. Frederick was sitting in the corner of my examining room, fully clothed with his hands deep in his pocket, his body turned away from me and avoiding eye contact. His body language betrayed his aversion of this conversation and a desire for anonymity.

His body was frozen, only the eyes, when asked a question, seemed to show any light, but a response was not quickly forthcoming. He looked rather small and underweight. He seemed very proper, meticulous in appearance but almost too controlled. He did not answer my question, "How are you?" but his eyes showed a profound sadness while he was looking towards his mother, expecting relief from her. Obviously, he was not going to volunteer any information. Faye, his mother, sighed and continued her story.

> He has always been a shy child. Even as an
> infant, he cried little, talked little and did
> not like to be kissed or hugged. He was
> potty trained early and never lost that
> sense of fastidiousness. But things have
> gotten worse since his grandmother died
> last Fall. She was the only person he would
> go to, talk to or just keep company while
> watching a TV program or reading a book.
> When she died, he hardly cried, but with-
> drew even more, staying in his room. I had
> to literally chase him outdoors to go and
> play, but often I found him alone sitting
> under a tree, staring in space. I know he
> was close to his grandmother, but he
> refused to talk to me about his feelings and
> never expressed his grief about her death.
> Now he has started to complain about joint
> pains in his hands and feet. My General
> Practitioner wants to put him on drugs, but
> the idea of medicating children shocks me.
> I hope you can do something, Doctor.

Out came the real triggering factor. The death of his beloved grandmother provided a clear window into
Frederick's emotional state. He behaved like the typical
"Water-Man:" he expresses his emotions with a profound-
ness one would hardly expect for a child of his age. Rather
than looking for consolation and expressing his feelings, he
shuts off the outside world and appears sulky and stubborn.
He does not even like conversations about himself and getting an answer from him is like pulling teeth. He will look
at his mother and expect her to give the answer for him, or
simply answer curtly with a "Yes" or "No." He is very self-
conscientious and careful, reflecting an early maturity and
fear of ridicule at the same time. He is very easily offended,
even at the slightest reprimand from his parents. This causes
him to withdraw in silent pain, leaving the adult unaware
of the hurt he has caused this very sensitive boy. And when
he cries, he does so more out of rage than from terror or
hurt. Don't try to soothe him, that will only make things
worse. You can very often stop the "Water-Boy's" crying if
you are sufficiently firm. Friends are few in his life. He is
cautious, and does not like to interact with a group like the
"Wood-Boy." He is so afraid of being hurt that he almost
seems emotionless. Nothing is further from the truth. The
"Water-Boy" is as sensitive as the "Heart-Boy," but while
the latter easily forgets and forgives, drifting to the next ex-
citable event in his life, the "Water-Boy" is "eternally" hurt.
It takes a long time before he releases his pent-up feelings.
If he does, it will not be by crying but sometimes by cling-
ing to his pets to which he feels very close. But he has a hard
time letting go of a sad event. While the "Heart-Child" will
openly cry over a sad event, and get distracted by the next
exciting event, the "Water-Child" dwells over the past, pon-

dering about how this could have been avoided and even questioning the extent to which he caused the event. It was no coincidence that Frederick came down with rheumatic pains. Suppressing his emotions like the "Metal-Man," the negative force of the emotional event becomes destructive on a physical level. Other physical expressions of his pent-up emotions are bed wetting and curiously, an inability to urinate in a public rest room. He is the child that learns to talk late. While this was a sign of general slowness in the "Earth-Boy," the "Water-Child" does not want to talk because of a grief. Don't forget that an emotional influence on the child starts in the womb. If the pregnant mother either undergoes an emotional trauma (divorce, separation) or does not want the child, but can't decide on an abortion because of her beliefs, then the child will be born a "Water-Child" with delayed talking as a consequence!

In Frederick's case, it was clear that grandmother's death, the closest and most trusted confident he had in his young life, triggered a deep grief in a susceptible boy. His physical pain in the joints was just a somatization of his deepest hurt. When his mother told me that he craved salt rather than sweet, I knew the remedy. His symptoms disappeared with a dose of Natrum muriaticum (sea salt). More importantly, he was able to come out of his shell and became the trusted confident of many of his class mates who liked his loyalty and wisdom. As for his mother, Faye, he soon became her favorite child. His sophistication and maturity increased his mother's pride in him. But Frederick was the big winner: the deep sadness had lifted and another dose of the same remedy fortified him so that another similar sad event would not have the same catastrophic impact.

The Teenager: Tormented and Isolated

There is no doubt that puberty, the time of growing up and moving away from the protectiveness of parents, is a hardship on almost any teenager. But there is no type who suffers more from increasing independence than the "Water-Teenager." The reserved, self-conscientious young man struggles with the newly acquired acne, reinforcing the already low self-image he has. He strives for perfection, an unobtainable goal, which creates severe anxiety and turmoil in the teenager's turbulent world. There is much less hardship for the other types. The "Liver-Wood-Teenager" finds his niche in his ever increasing popularity and enjoys his long yearned for sense of independence. The "Heart-Teenager" might suffer his first heartbreak but is caught up with many other thrilling projects. Music, dancing, theater and his natural lively personality provide many outlets for his pent-up energy. The "Earth-Boy" might reach puberty later (everything takes time for him) and he grows into the soft, popular polar bear, loved at school and at home. The "Metal-Teenager" is the closest to the "Water-Teenager" with his sense of justice and suppressing of his feelings. The biggest difference is that the "Metal-Boy" has a tendency to get physically sick while the "Water-Boy" is more emotionally than physically off balance. Alas, calamity can easily occur in the "Water-Teenager" when sad events happen to him. The next clinical case from my practice illustrates this so well.

> I am here with my son Paul, Doctor. Paul
> suffers from anorexia nervosa. Look at him.
> He has lost so much weight; eating is a
> struggle and yet you can't reason with him.

> My husband and I have sent him to a
> specialized clinic on the East coast. As long
> as he is there under supervision, he does
> relatively well. But the moment he is left on
> his own, he relapses to the same behavior. I
> am afraid he is killing himself and nobody
> seems to be able to do something perma-
> nent.

Anorexia nervosa and bulimia are two devastating eating disorders, often starting during the turbulent puberty
years. Western medicine is frequently at a loss regarding its
origin and institutes. As happens so often in most of these
cases, there is a prescribed similar therapy. Therapy consists of hospitalizing these unfortunate victims from 1 to 2
years, while controlling them with psychotropic medications. Repeatedly I have seen that everything goes well as
long as they are in the hospital, but once they enter society
again many of them fail to win the battle against this "de-
mon." Why? Because of Western medicine's inability to in-
dividualize and match the disease picture with the correct
remedy. For most mental diseases, homeopathy is by far
superior to Western medicine: every patient is not put into a
category for diagnosis, the name of disease is not even per-
tinent. What is important is the clinical picture and above
all, the origin of the disease. Why is this teenager behaving
this way? What happened in his life when his illness started?
This was the clue in Paul's case too.

> Everything started when he was 12 years-
> old, Doctor. His father and I divorced at
> that time and Paul came to live with me
> full-time. He was very close to his father

and although his father visited him quite frequently, I have a hunch that he never got over the separation. Now he seems to be angry at his father, who he blames, but sometimes he blames himself for the separation. And as much as I try to comfort him, he does not want to hear it. He isolates himself, does not participate much in social events at school and I don't even think he has one good friend.

The divorce could not have come at a worse time for Paul. The sensitive, struggling teenager is hit by a tornado of grief and insecurity while he is trying to adjust to the most difficult period in his life. Beware parents, if you have a "Water-Child," that the death of a family member or a friend, a separation or divorce, or the loss of a good friend at school (moving away for instance), will be experienced to a much greater degree of sadness by him than you would ever expect. Frequently, a deterioration of mental and physical health sets in, landing the lost teenager in the deepest abyss of melancholy and depression. The "Water-Teenager," more than any other type, blames himself unjustifiably for the sad event that happened. He feels that he must be the cause of the divorce, his friend moved away because he does not want to be with him and grandmother died because of him. Tormenting thoughts, but so real for an unbalanced teenager. He shuts down by building a defensive wall—his way of protecting himself. He cannot possibly stand to be hurt like that again. Amazingly enough, he can hold grudges forever and will have a hard time forgiving. Paul's sadness was mixed with anger towards his father for leaving him. His anorexia was the ultimate protest on one hand and a sacrifice to admit his "guilt" on the other hand.

While anorexia nervosa and bulimia are often linked to grief and heartbreak (especially in the "Water" type), other incidents trigger this so often deadly disease. Indignation is a major factor. Either the child's dignity has been taken away at school, when he was unjustly punished and ridiculed in front of the class, or the mental, emotional, verbal and sexual abuse happened at home where one of the parents is dysfunctional and dictatorial. The child is abused by the very people he trusted and loved the most. He must be very bad indeed to deserve this and starving himself to death seems to be an appropriate punishment. We should not forget the millions of households in which children have to deal with alcoholic parents. Someone like Paul will feel that it is up to him to save the rest of the family and takes on the responsibility for the behavior of the irresponsible parent. Guilt and remorse will stay with him forever. I have seen all these triggering factors in my practice. The beauty of homeopathy is that each case is individualized and receives, besides counseling, an appropriate homeopathic remedy without side effects.

It is not hard to imagine that a "Water-Child" has a lot of fears. The biggest fear, of course, is fear of abandonment. As in Paul's case, he continually had to know where his mother was going if she left the house and when would she be back, "Please don't be late." Having seen one of the parents "walk" out of his life, through divorce, he fears that the other parent will do the same. He feels he is a burden, the guilty party. Why then wouldn't his mother decide one day to just leave him behind? Don't tell him, "Stop behaving like a baby." He will say nothing, withdraw to his room and sulk. And long after you forgot about the incident, he will hold this pain deep in his heart, fueled, unfortunately, by the next minor incident. Don't expect to be able to hold him in your arms and console him. He will have no part of it because he is convinced that you don't understand him. In fact nobody does, so why talk about it. Imagine the demanding, yelling "Wood-Parent" who fumes at this show of "stubbornness and rebellion." It reinforces the feeling in the teenager that no one understands the depth of his pain. Other fears are abundant. Fear of being alone, of public speaking (he does not want to have the attention), of robbers, of dying and of insects.

Paul's condition was dramatically improved with a dose of Natrum muriaticum. There was no need for further drugs and hospitalization. And communication with his mother and friends became open and friendly. The wonder of "sea salt!"

The Adult: The Reformer and Perfectionist

One of the most bizarre, yet most rewarding cases in my practice was the history of a 35 year-old teacher. The interesting fact was that he had been my Mother's student when she was a kindergarten teacher in Belgium, and she basically saw all the village children as they came through her classroom. It proved to be of great value to me in his therapy. But let's hear what Richard said as he had presented himself to me twenty years ago.

The Man Who Couldn't Stop Cleaning

Dr. Luc, I have a problem that is not only costing me my health, but is destroying my family life as well. I have two little children and a dear wife, but I am afraid I am going to lose them. The problem is, I am a cleaning and control freak. When my little girls come home, I want to help them hang their coats up but it takes me four hours before I am satisfied with the result. We basically live in the kitchen because my family knows that they can't touch anything in the living room. If they pick up the phone, I catch myself cleaning it with a towel. If they move a vase, I can't stop myself from trying to put it back in the same place. I find myself cleaning my car in the middle of the night. When I wash my hands before dinner, I scrub them so hard that they become raw. Of course, I am dead tired in the morning, but I can't stop myself. And don't tell me to go to the psychiatrist. I have been there and his drugs did not help at all.

I could see the terror his family was going through and what an ordeal it was for him, too. He felt very guilty about bringing his family to such a deplorable state. Socializing was impossible (they never got out of the door on time) and Richard realized he was traumatizing his wife and children. But neither his love for his family, nor his own deteriorating energy could overcome the devastating pull of his "cleaning alter-ego," as he called it. No doubt, he was diagnosed with Obsessive Compulsive Disorder (OCD): his rituals, his aggressive obsessions, his need for symmetry, order and exactness, his rearranging his girls' coats were all telltale signs of a compulsive personality disorder, as his psychiatrist had stated so well. The problem was that the few drugs available, Anafranil, and Lithium, were of no help. The newer medications, Prozac and Zoloft, were not yet available, but I doubt that they would have helped. He tried behavior therapy, especially what his therapist called, "exposure with response prevention," in which he was forced to shake hands with perfect strangers on the street without being allowed to wash his hands till later that night. It was an utter failure. As he was telling me this, his fear of contamination was very obvious.

> When I tuck my girls in at night, I wear a
> sterile mask for fear of infecting them. And
> I force my wife to do the same thing. I
> sterilize everything that comes into my
> grasp and boil water twice before using it
> for fear of contamination.

This concern with germs is, of course, part of his make-up. Richard had concern for body wastes and secretions (he definitely did not want to use someone else's toilet) and he had an excessive concern about chemical and environmental contamination. His children were never sent to summer camp. They would not survive there, according to Richard. While I doubted that they would survive at home if something was not done soon for Richard. Organic vegetables were peeled and scrubbed for an hour straight and no raw fruits were eaten. Period. Cleanliness was the center of attention. It made me think of another real-life case I had. That patient told me that he wanted to commit suicide. Like any "Water-Man" he was very meticulous in preparing for his death and, of course, it was going to be done in a *clean* way.

No blood running all over by slitting his wrists, no gun splattering his brains out; the very thought would make him shudder. He intended to commit suicide by putting his head in the gas oven. While he was doing so, he noticed that the oven was greasy. He started to clean it and forgot all about committing suicide. I must admit, I had difficulty trying not to smile. But let's return to Richard.

As I mentioned before, luck was on my side in trying to discover his exciting factor. My mother saw him when he was a five year-old kid. He stood out in her memory because he was the kid that was always dressed to a Tee. A little suit and tie (at three years of age!) and he never did participate in the "dirty" games such as soccer like other children. He would clean his little table before and after school. He was shy, reserved and considered strange and a nerd by other children. No doubt he was born a "Water-Child," the one type that will have this disorder more than anyone else. His mother was the other "cleanliness freak." No doubt she instilled in him the routine but at the same time this also suggested a hereditary factor, or miasm, in homeopathy. I was curious when it had gotten out of hand. Richard complied by relating the following:

> When I was seventeen, I went to the
> Middle East on vacation with friends. We
> all got sick with travelers' diarrhea.
> Strangely enough after that, my cleansing
> habits became exaggerated to the point
> where I am right now. While my friends
> seem to have had no consequences, I found
> myself overwhelmed by a growing concern
> about germs and parasites. I have never
> been well since then.

This was the straw that broke the camel's back for Richard. For me it was the clue to the right remedy: "Never well since travelers' diarrhea" responds to Arsenicum (poison treats poison!). This incident implanted on a constitutional "Water-Man" frequently leads to OCD. Whereas his fear of "bugs" was somewhat controlled before, this infection took his Vital Energy completely out of balance. For a homeopathic physician, diagnosis and therapy in this case is fairly simple since the remedy Arsenicum has in its "provings", or testing, symptoms of both diarrhea and compulsive hand washing. Since "Like Cures Like" the conclusion is evident.

> You know, Doctor, I am happy to tell you that since I took that homeopathic remedy two months ago, everything is going so much better. We have even been on a short family vacation, something we had not done in ten years. I am again full of hope. I am much less compulsive and we now have dinner in our dining room. I never thought I could manage to do that. Whatever these little pills are, just give me some more to take home. I see the end of the tunnel now. What's the name of these pellets again?

There was one thing I did not do with Richard that I do with every patient: divulge the name of the remedy. I told him it was Sac. lac. (which stands for sugar lactose, the equivalent of the placebo of Western medicine). You can imagine what telling him that his remedy was Arsenic (in homeopathic doses) would do to him with his fear of dying and disease. His already extreme fears would prevent him from taking it. I was very pleased to see that for the many years I knew his family, he stayed a stable "Water-Man." Still punctual, detailed in his work and clean in his manners and attire, but not more so than millions of other people.

The Man Who Wanted to Die Since He Was Three Years-Old

There are few emotions as strong as the will to survive. The most fundamental instinct of mankind is self preservation. Hence, the impulse to kill one's self is the deepest aberration and mental distortion against the powerful survival instinct present in any living being. Therefore the next story is a heartbreaking one as Charles, 70 years-old, had struggled against this feeling all his life.

> I was born the seventh child (an "Oh, not again!"). My father died when I was 18 months-old. I was always afraid. When I was three years old, I wanted to die and be with my dad. My older sister and I argued about who would be the first to die and be with dad. When she did die at age 30, she said to me "I'll be with dad first." My older sister had to take care of me because mom was told that we would be taken away. So she worked hard and I felt alone. My sister, one year older, and I stuck together like glue, afraid and hoping we could die. No one ever mentioned what happened to dad. When I was 11 years-old, I took a job as a baby-sitter. I felt like everyone had to work

hard because of me. I still wonder why I
am here. I wonder who I am. I feel unwanted.

A tragic story indeed. First of all, Charles was an after-
thought in the family and came "accidentally" into this
world. That must have implanted a sense of not being
wanted from birth on. We know in homeopathy, that if the
mother has an unwanted pregnancy but cannot or does not
want to abort, that the child is born feeling the heartbreak
and the helplessness of the mother. But the death of the father apparently put the whole family into a spin. Charles
was only 18 months-old when he felt "abandoned" by his
father. From then on, he and his sister had only one wish: to
be with dad, even if this meant dying. His feelings of loneliness and abandonment increased when his mom was forced
to take a job and leave her family to fend for themselves.
This created a deep feeling of guilt in Charles who felt that
if it was not for him, none of this would have happened.
What a way for a young boy to feel. It was so intense that
even at age 70, he still felt unwanted and unsure about his
destiny on earth.

Unfortunately, his feelings of heartbreak and abandonment were duplicated a little later in his life, reinforcing this
feeling of unworthiness.

After dad died, my oldest sister told me
that if I cried, she would make larger and
larger ghost shadows on the wall. I guess
she hated me. When I was 5 years-old, my
mother planned to remarry. Her husband-
to-be looked a lot like my dad. I thought he
was my dad and wanted him to come to

> me. He refused, I guess he did not know
> how to handle children. So my mom threw
> him out. She said to him, "You are breaking
> his heart." My mom said that afterwards I
> sat on the floor and wouldn't talk to any-
> one for days. I felt more unwanted.

First there was his older sister who forced Charles to suppress his feelings, something opposite to his nature. He told me he liked consolation, that he was very shy, easily hurt and that even now, he held back his tears. But the real shocker was the incident with the surrogate father-to-be. The impressionable Charles was sure this was his father "born again" who came back to take finally care of him and the rest of the family. Imagine this second similar heartbreak situation happening to this fragile boy. An earthquake could not have hit harder. Indeed, Charles' sense of unworthiness lasted up until the time we met. He did not fill out the rest of his questionnaire because he stated,

> I can't say anything more because it hurts
> too much. I just want to mention that I have
> bizarre dreams. I dream that I fall in a deep
> hole and wake up with wondering, "Why
> are we here?"

The fears in the "Water-Man" are many. But the number one fear, almost as in the "Heart-Man," is the fear of abandonment. We already mentioned the fear of contamination in the previous case: the fear of catching germs from some-one else dominates his life. I felt sad that Charles had to wait until he was 70 years-old before he got help. Of course his shyness and utter loneliness shut him off from the rest of the world. I could only imagine what his life could have been like if he had received the proper homeopathic remedy 65 years ago instead of now. I gave him Pulsatilla (Windflower) and this is what he told me.

> When I took the first dose, I felt a strong throbbing in the bridge of my nose for five minutes. Then a stream of saliva came down into the roof of my mouth and ran steadily for a few minutes. It felt very soothing. I started to cry. My nose ran for a long time. The second week, I felt very relaxed, but I wanted to rest all the time. Pimples started appearing on my body, the calluses on my feet have diminished about 75% now and they are peeling off fast. My feet are of a better color and I have feeling in them. My thinking has changed. I don't get hurt so easily. I want to thank you. I am feeling much better.

A remarkable cure of such an old case in such a short time (one month!). Almost immediately after the first dose his body started to respond with a physical and emotional improvement. The curious thing was how his body started cleansing so fast (throbbing, nose running, shedding of calluses, appearance of pimples) as if it finally decided after all these years to clean up. This is a true cure in homeopathy as the disease has to go from the interior to the exterior. Of course that took energy and he stated that he felt rather tired during that first week. But the mental improvement was there too: he felt much more relaxed and he was not easily offended anymore. The degree of hurt diminished rapidly.

Could you blame me for feeling sad that Charles had never had the opportunity to take that same inexpensive, non-toxic Windflower when he needed it as a child? His life indeed would have been totally different and richer. Charles kept improving on the same remedy until he finally could stop taking it after five months. Life for Charles started at age 70!

The Mind Wants, the Body Refuses

My chief complaint is a lack of energy, Doctor. My muscles are sore and tired. I feel a strong mental frustration because my mind is often willing and active, especially in the morning. Upon rising I become very frustrated when I physically don't have the energy to carry out all the activities my mind has planned. I am emotionally unhappy with my poor performance on many levels. I was diagnosed with Chronic Fatigue Syndrome.

Just another case of unsolvable CFIDS or was a virus responsible for Werner's situation? Let's follow his history to find out.

My problem began in February 1988 following an acute viral illness. Up till then, I felt 100% fit. One morning I got out of bed and collapsed. I had a fever, no appetite for food only for cold drinks. I was unable to walk for even a few yards! I had hallucinations with a fever of 103°F. I stayed in bed for ten days. I was tested for several viruses with negative results. This viral attack occurred on and off for the next 12 months. I am aggravated by a lack of sleep (I must be in bed by 8 p.m.) and need an afternoon nap. There are so many activities I used to enjoy doing that I can no longer actively participate in—gardening, walks to the beach, cooking, or just strolling in the mall. And I have a complete lack of concentration and a poor memory.

Sounds like a perfect case of Chronic Fatigue, and this time linked to a viral infection. But how did his Vital Energy decrease so much as to allow the unknown virus (nothing was cultured adding to the confusion for his therapy) to change Werner from a fit, able man to a mere shadow of himself overnight, not capable of even walking a few yards?

Before this first attack started, we had just come back from an island vacation. While we were there, the weather, unfortunately, was not good: damp, rainy, cold. I felt responsible for my family and worried about them not having a good time. Two days after I returned I had this first attack. And since then, I have never felt the same.

Apparently, a relentless attack of Damp-Cold coupled with worry had decreased Werner's Vital Energy sufficiently to allow the virus to strike with such ferocity. It was not just simple fatigue as he talked about a sudden collapse. Werner was 35 years-old, and rarely do we find a patient of this age who has not been subjected to previous traumas.

> I had four engagements prior to being
> married, three of which I called off. The
> first one was to a woman five years older. I
> discovered she had been unfaithful during
> our engagement. I was emotionally shat-
> tered by this event and it took at least 3
> years to get over this heartbreak. Unfortu-
> nately I started drinking during this time
> and I struggled with alcohol for ten years. I
> have been dry now for two years.

As usual when I hear such a story, the pity is that no
immediate cure was instituted for the heartbreak or the al-
coholism. His own Vital Energy was used to bring him back
to a fragile balance, a balance that was broken by the first
exposure of cold-dampness. It became clear to me that he
became a "Water-Man" after this last event as he explained
his fears to me.

> The biggest stress factor I have right now in
> my life is my fear that I am never going to
> get better. I am so anxious about having my
> former energy levels restored that I don't
> believe anyone can help me anymore.
> Doctors keep on testing me because I ask
> them to do so, but all test results are nega-
> tive. Maybe I am suffering from a disease
> that is as yet unknown. My disease is
> probably worse than anything you have
> seen, Doctor. I am afraid I am going to die
> from this condition. Do you think that you

should do your own testing just to make
sure the other doctors did not miss anything?

No other type has as many phobias as the "Water-Man."
He has the greatest anxiety about his health and suspects
that he suffers from many, incurable, yet to-be-discovered
diseases. There is no bigger hypochondriac (in homeopathy
this is NOT the derogatory term it is in Western medicine)
and he has read as much as possible about his disease. He is
more open than anyone else to new therapies since he is
fascinated with tests. He will demand that some tests he
has heard of be performed or even that previous tests be
repeated since he is convinced that the other ones were not
accurate. This is the patient who needs to be seen at once.
His despair is great since he is suffering from "a serious disease" so he should be seen the same day. The "Water-Man"
will send in advance a detailed list (pages long!) describing
his illness, together with many copies of tests already performed. He will demand that the physician read these pages
before he comes for his appointment because there is so
much more he wants to discuss.

A "Water-Man" needs to be pushed out the door of the
physician's consultation room because he is convinced he
has not yet explained everything . When he finally leaves,
holding the door knob, he says: "By the way, did I tell you
about this symptom and that test . . ." This is not the last his
doctor has heard from him. When the physician comes to
his office in the morning, he finds his answering machine
filled with one long message from the same patient because
he just "thought about another symptom." First the doctor
is berated on the machine since "He does not like to talk to a
machine, he wants to talk to a real person." A machine is

very cold and especially time-limiting, something a "Water-Man" hates. His disease is the most important event in this world, so he is not grateful when his physician takes a vacation. Of course, he will try to convince his doctor that he needs to know where he is going to be on vacation since most likely "his disease is going to take a turn for the worse while the doctor is gone." God forbid if the physician does relay this information. He is sure to get a daily report from this "Water-Man."

Of course he loves a homeopathic physician who listens for an hour to each new patient, probing for intimate details. Even more, he loves the concept of a holistic center where he can consult with anyone present there. And he is sure to remark that all the doctors should get together to discuss this mysterious case of his. And guess what the topic of conversation is among friends: either his or your illness. By now he considers himself somewhat of a doctor and has enormous sympathy for any diseased person. He weeps easily when others talk about their diseases since he has no difficulty putting himself in other people's shoes, identifying with their sorrow and pain. His phobias are not limited to disease, cancer and dying. The "Water-Man" has more phobias than any other type. Agoraphobia, fear of public speaking, heights, narrow spaces, flying, dentists, claustrophobia, etc. Of course there is an immense concern for the family, as we have seen in the "Earth-Man." But the "Water-Man" is full of future disasters and is sure that his children were involved in a car crash when they are five minutes late. They force their children to dress well (imagine the "Water-Parent" struggling with the hot "Liver-Boy!") out of fear they will get that next dreadful cold that is waiting around the corner. Because doom and gloom *will* happen, it is just a question of *when*. They are worriers about health related issues and therefore it is natural for them to be "health nuts." They cook only in the right kind of pot, eat only organic food and have an inclination to be vegetarian. Werner had become a "Water-Man." His disease consumed his life, he feared for the future and no one was going to be able to help him. It is almost an irony that the "Killer who cures," as we call Arsenicum in homeopathy, relieved his extreme anxiety while restoring his physical fitness. True to a "Water-Man" it was his wife who first told me of the vast improvement she had seen in her husband. Werner himself was still concentrating on the 10% of the remaining symptoms, rather than on the 90% cured.

You have met some of the different shades of the "Water-Man." To summarize them emotionally:

The "Water-Man"

Frugal, meticulous, over prepared, anxious, full of phobias, fastidious, critical, worry wart, elegant, good taste, perfectionist, vindictive, selfish, competitive, intelligent, arrogant, self-disciplined, ambitious, proud, sentimental, private, introvert, taciturn, gloomy, hypochondriac, refined, eye for detail and impatience for tardiness and mediocrity.

A classical example of the "Water-Man" is Sherlock Holmes, the famous private investigator. Always prepared to the maximum, with a keen eye for details. He rightly coined the phrase, "That which is out of the common, usually leads to the solution of the case." He was ambitious and proud, but rightly, he was the best. The Belgian detective, Hercule Poirot, in Agatha Christie's novels, is another fine example. Always sophisticated, elegant, polite, the true gentleman and very methodical in resolving his cases. He does not put himself at the center of attention but has that effect anyway through his presence, his wittiness and sharp deduction powers. No matter the weather, he is always impeccably dressed and seems to be in control even at the most unexpected moments. Great reformers and crusaders in history, like Ghandi, are "Water" types. They are the people protesting conditions accepted as familiar inconveniences, fighting against the selfish arrogance of employers who consider the poor workers as disposable machines on hire, and confronting the political paralysis in economic crises.

Other professions, besides private investigators, in which the "Water" type are numerous are secretaries, inspectors, book editors, landscape designers, interior designers, professors, psychotherapists, librarians, optometrists, dentists, social workers, graphic designers, bankers, and pharmacists. All of these professions rely on integrity, self-discipline and a willingness to spend much time on detail work. A good secretary likes her 9 to 5 job, although she will take work home if necessary. As anyone who works in an office knows, give a job that needs to be done quickly to the person that is the busiest. When you select a secretary, make sure to choose a "Water" person: dependable, neat, highly organized, polite, correct with people, and feelings of indignation when people come late for their appointment or forget to pay. The "Water- Secretary" will take this personally. S/he expects from you, the client, exactly the same that she stands for: integrity, dependability and following the rules. If you fail to pass this test, the "Water-Person" has nothing but contempt for you and will tell you so with a directness that stings. A message to the boss of this 'Water-Secretary:" promote this person on time. The "Water-Person" knows he is good and has a strong sense of what is "owed" him. This easily turns into indignation when deprived of career advantages.

The academic world is full of these "Water-Teachers." They are always over prepared, very meticulous and stick rigorously to details. They have their whole schedule outlined and don't like to deviate one iota from it. They can have nightmares before they start a new class thinking they did not prepare *enough*. Of course, they expect exactly the same from their students. Quite the contrary to the "Wood-Teacher" who is eloquent, bombastic, scholastic and sometimes overwhelms his students with an avalanche of facts and stories. Quite different, too, from the "Fire-Teacher" who is very enthusiastic, loquacious, spontaneous, creative and inspirational, sometimes jumping from one subject to another.

Most psychotherapists belong to this type. For one, many have been called to the profession by their own life experience of grief and heartbreak which figures prominently in this type. They love to "dwell" over the past with their patients, sometimes taking many years before progress is made. They are perfect for people who have undergone the same kind of heartbreak, *as long as the patient reacts in the same fashion to this grief*: with hidden grief (only brought up with the psychotherapist), vindictiveness, unforgiving, desirous of sympathy yet averse to and aggravated by consolation, never forgetting people who have formerly given offense and with a new goal in life, reforming this world. Of course you will find therapists in other prototypes. The "Earth-Psychotherapist" is more like a mother to her client: gentle, understanding, unconditionally supporting, always in tune with the wishes of the client, patient and down-to-earth. But the "Water" type is more prevalent in this profession.

We have already found the homeopathic physician in the "Wood" type. Many of them find a place here, too. It takes much perseverance, an eye for detail, and patience to sift through tons of material (lab tests, diagnoses, symptoms) to find the needle in the haystack. Most of the best homeopaths will be a combination of "Wood-Water:" he loves to organize and collect the mountain of evidence and organize it in precise, clear and logical language. Dr. Samuel Hahnemann, the father of homeopathy, was such a person. He spent his entire life postulating the laws and principles of homeopathy and succeeded by doing something that no other human being in history has been able to do: complete the study of one science in one's lifetime. It took the sense of collector and studiousness of the "Wood-Man" combined with the discipline, the perseverance and single-mindedness of the "Water-Man." Humankind is eternally indebted to this man.

The Physical Characteristics of the "Water-Man"

Physically, this "Water-Man" is a race horse: thin, nervous, restless and sometimes with an angry disposition. Rarely will you find obese people among this type (the Earth types and to a lesser degree the Metal types). They are tall and slender, with a tendency to walk very erect, head up, reflecting their proud manner. The unbalanced "Water-Man", on the other hand, is timid, walking around with his head down as if to conceal his eyes. If he looks you in the eye, it is short-lasting as if to hide his deepest painful emotions.

He is the one with the allergic shiners: black circles under the eyes if he is out of balance. The color black corresponds to this type (they love to dress in black or white) and is found under the eyes when the adrenals are not functioning well. This happens often as this type is full of anxiety and insecurity about the future, putting stress on his hard-functioning adrenals. When he wilts under pressure (which does not happen quickly as he has a lot of determination), he starts walking with his head stooped and spinal column bent forward. Often you can find edema, or water collection, in the eyelids (the lower especially) or under the eyes, which the Chinese called "chamber of tears." This is especially obvious in the morning, indicating a weak detoxification function of the kidney.

The seriousness of his face is accentuated by a sharp, eagle-like nose. Often he wears "intellectual looking" glasses and has a thin mustache. The "Water-Man" can give the impression of being very emotional, as if tears are ready at any moment. He almost looks pathetic, never sure if he wants to open his heart to the person listening to him and ready to withdraw from the first little hurt he suspects. It is not an arrogant look, not a penetrating, dominating one like the "Wood-Man." Rather, a look which sizes up the other person to see if he can dare to expose his deepest feelings. The lips are often oval, pursed and pinched, as if he is continually hiding disapproval. His words are delayed by reflective selectivity. It all adds up to an impression of a tight personality. His hands are short and feel soft, almost as if they contain water.

The "Water-Man" is very chilly. His idea of winter, his notion of cold, is when the mercury dips down into the low fifties. Therefore, he hates winter which is more a period of hibernation. It is a time for him to sleep in, go to bed early and a general tendency to not leave home. The cold is especially felt in his limbs: his feet and hands are always ice cold. He is the one proclaiming to feel the cold penetrating his bones. He is rather fragile and subject to frequent diseases.

Often he projects a picture of general exhaustion which never seems to leave him.

This "Water" type prefers, by far, salty things above sweet ones. He will always add salt to his food and loves salty meats like salami, ham, bacon, etc. His favorite color is black. Malfunctioning of the kidney and bladder is reflected on the lower, deeper part of the tongue: the more sluggish the excretion, the thicker and more yellow the fur on the lower third of the tongue.

The "Water-Man" and His Diseases

The child looks a little like the "Metal-Boy." But rather than the lungs, his vulnerable area is the tonsils. They are continuously infected, almost always leading to a tonsillectomy. Not rarely, an inadequately treated tonsillitis leads to juvenile rheumatoid arthritis, a typical constitutional disease of this type. It does not surprise the acupuncturist who knows the link between the organ kidney and the bones in general. The child is usually fragile and sad. It is very common to see the same predisposition in the mother of this "Water-Boy." His mother frequently suffers from arthritis, especially rheumatoid, and in her history we often find sad, heartbreaking events proceeding this auto-immune disorder. As an adolescent, the "Water" type suffers emotionally the most of all the types: hypersensitive, unhappy with the surrounding world, and withdrawn. There are often physical repercussions: puberty starts later in these children and enuresis nocturna (bed wetting) can last till a later age.

The adult's diseases are linked to the kidney and bladder. Recurrent urinary infections, bladder incontinence, albuminuria, urinary stone formations, edema under the eyes, and kidney diseases like pyelonephritis (infection of the kidneys). The Chinese linked the kidney organ to the bones. The "Water-Man" has a very weak back and complains often about stiffness, soreness and back-breaking pains in the lower back (lumbago). More than any other type he will be subjected to the agonizing pain of slipped discs, always aggravated by exposure to cold-dampness. Other "bone diseases" frequently encountered in this type are osteoporosis, early tooth caries, Bechterew's disease and osteoarthritis throughout the body. The worst positions for the "Water-Man" are standing and sitting for a long time. They need to move around in order to relieve stiffness and pain.

For the Chinese, kidneys are also linked to the ears. A typical sign of deficient working kidneys is ringing of the ears, or tinnitus. Meniere's disease with tinnitus, vertigo and fullness of the ear is a "Water-Man's" disease. So are hearing impairment and vertigo.

The whole sexual apparatus is dependent on the kidney energy. The kidneys, together with the liver, are most important for a normal sexual life. Impotence, sterility, frigidity and general lack of sexual desire is often encountered in the "Water-Man." He often suffers from loss of sperm during the night (spermatorrhea).

Prostate problems seem to be increasing at an alarming rate. By the age of 60, 50% of all men suffer from some form of prostate dysfunction. Burning urination, getting up two or three times at night to urinate, pressing pains in the bladder, inability to empty the bladder, bladder urgency, and a weak urinary stream are just some of the symptoms. Very often, if untreated and undetected, these problems can lead to prostate cancer. Again, more than any other type, the "Water-Man" needs to be aware of the symptoms and warning signs of prostate cancer. Due to his inherent weakness, he will often suffer from this disease.

Although diabetes is linked to the "Earth" type, we should clarify that it is mainly Adult Onset Diabetes, non dependent on insulin, which belongs to this type. The diabetes of the thin people, dependent on intake of insulin, is more a disease of the "Water" type.

Chinese medicine teaches us, too, that the hair on the head is dependent on a good "Kidney" energy, one of the organs belonging to the element Water. Loss of hair, either in bunches or only in certain places, like Alopecia areata, has to be linked to a disruption of this Kidney energy. The biggest triggering factors, as we see in these "Water" cases presented, are sudden fright, continuous fear, heart break, financial worry and worry about health.

We have seen that the "Heart" type is the one susceptible to environmental sensitivities. But the "Water-Man" is the one with the incessant food allergies. It is interesting to see that both the "Heart- and Water-Man" are subject to heartbreak. While a "Heart-Man" reacts mainly with psychological consequences (depression, melancholy, hysteria, neuroses), the "Water-Man" often feels the impact of heartbreak on his body: rheumatoid arthritis, Muscular Sclerosis, diabetes, bone problems in general, food allergies and prostate cancer can be linked to this trauma. Because Western medicine only looks at the end result, and omits to link the emotional trauma to the physical consequence, many of these "Water" diseases go untreated or are poorly treated. It is up to the reader to work together with his physician to find a clue to many of these "mystery diseases."

How Did He Become a "Water-Man?"

You already met some of the "Water-Men" in previous cases. You met Richard, who was hereditarily predestined and aggravated by food poisoning; Charles who became a "Water-Man" through a lack of love and the feeling of being unwanted; and Werner, who changed into the fearful "Water" type because of a viral infection, catching the "germ phobia" so classic of this type. Heredity, lack of love, viral infections and food poisoning are just some of the triggering factors able to transform someone into a "Water-Man." The next cases will explain more about some of the well-known and lesser known "Water" etiologic factors.

Abandoned as a Child, Fatigued as an Adult

I am constantly fatigued, Doctor. I have to force myself to do anything. Sometimes it seems like too much effort to watch TV, but if I do nothing, my mind goes around in circles. I get exhausted just from vacuuming the house. At night, I feel tired but not sleepy. Consequently, I am often awake during the night, and half asleep for most of the day. When you add that to the fact that I can't grasp more than a couple of facts at the time, and I forget things I was going to say, then you can see that it is no surprise that my boss wants to fire me. When I remember one thing and try to grasp more, what I already have slips away. It is utterly frustrating and impossible to live with, Doctor. Other doctors have called it Chronic Fatigue, depression, anxiety, and

hysteria. Maybe they know more about
diseases than I do, but as far as a cure is
concerned, I am on my own. Thousands of
dollars and years later, I am still the same.

This was a history that I have heard so many times, and
certainly was going to hear many more times, in my practice. Patients lost in a flood of symptoms, in an unknown
disease that seemed to suck the last energy they have, drain
their financial coffers and leave their doctors with their hands
up in the air. Blood tests are performed; some show absolutely no abnormalities, some show a wave of abnormal
numbers of common viruses, yeast cells and bacteria, but
the result is always the same. The patient does his "tour" of
doctors until he himself breaks the vicious circle, either because he is broke, or he finally realizes that his doctors are
doing more hoping and praying than curing. Devastating
indeed and, depending on the type of man, their reactions
will be different. The "Liver-Man" will continuously keep
challenging his doctors by doing a great amount of self-
study; the "Heart-Man" tries to make the best of it and often remains cheerful even under the worst circumstances.
The "Earth-Man" is more concerned with not being able to
take care of his own family than with his own health and as
usual, proceeds with caution and slowness. The "Metal-
Man" often becomes depressed and fearful about the future,
although till the bitter end, he will follow the guidelines set
forth by his doctors. The "Water-Man" is overwhelmed with
fears about his health and will keep changing doctors, healing modalities and clinics, and in the end is often labeled a
"hypochondriac," with whom no one wants to deal. Before
we as doctors use this word, we should sink our teeth into
the case, exploring every detail of the patient's life, imagin-

ing ourselves as Sherlock Holmes, excited, not overwhelmed, by a difficult, mysterious case. In Frank's case I decided to do just that. He was only 34 years-old, far too young to be in such a sorry state.

> My health started to deteriorate when I started school at age 6. I hated school. I felt defenseless and abandoned in a hostile world in which I did not know how to cope. I was in a constant state of tension, felt sick every morning and could hardly eat. I guess it did not help me that when I was born my parents were house parents to 16 other kids. Mom was extremely tense and exhausted before and after birth and could not breast-feed. At times I wanted attention or to be fed, but she could not comply since she always had other things to do. When I was 4 years-old, my cat was killed and I remember being heartbroken! Two more pets died when I was 6 and 7. Each time, I was told I had been heartbroken. I really worried over school work. Even in the first grade things that were said to other kids about not working hard enough I took to heart, and really feared I would not be promoted. It got worse when I was twelve. I was acutely anxious over every minor test and was often upset and crying over homework. I really felt I could not cope. That same year I experienced several bouts of tonsillitis.

After you have read the previous pages, you can see the proto-type emerging. Abandonment was an early issue in this sensitive child. The mother was a burnt-out "Earth" type who would have benefited enormously from the homeopathic remedy Sepia (in addition to a well-deserved vacation!). The heartbreaks were multiplied when, in succession, his three cats died. The "Water" type, above all, loves cats, so this was not a minor event in his life. And in school he became a true "Water-Man." He never felt prepared enough, always worrying about not doing well and failing the next test. This anxiety of failure was never resolved, finally having an impact on his physical health. The typical "Water" tonsillitis appeared, getting progressively worse over the years. It did not help that Franks' love life was more like a rocking boat on heavy seas than smooth sailing in balmy weather.

> I definitely got even worse and more
> preoccupied when I was in love and
> planned to marry. The wedding was
> planned for the summer but I was jilted in
> April. I felt devastated and depressed. That
> was the straw that broke the camel's back.
> Now I am easily upset, overreact to little
> things, am easily hurt, impatient, irritable,
> frustrated and constantly worried and
> tense about anything and everything. I feel
> if someone is upset that it must be my fault.
> I take criticism meant for other people. I
> have started feeling that I will never get
> well. I am more resigned and apathetic
> about my situation now.

This broken love affair was devastating to Frank, even more so because he is a "Water-Man." From a young age on, the "Water-Man" will cultivate a romantic and perfect love picture. A picture of one and only one great absolute love. All his life, he will carry this ideal picture of love. More than any other type, he is monogamous and loyal. He demands perfection in love from himself and his partner. He will be totally devastated by his partner's infidelity, as happened in Frank's case. For him there is only a once-in-a-lifetime great love, and it will be difficult for the "Water-Man" to give himself totally a second chance. Often, after he is hurt like Frank was, he becomes a victim of his painful destiny. He sighs, cries in silence, hold grudges and complains easily. Frequently he is overwhelmed with guilt. Many times, nature is his escape for his profound sadness. It is there that he finds serenity and detachment from this cruel world. There is a state of loneliness and isolation, accentuated by a longing for sympathy from others. He resigns himself to be dejected and pessimistic, killing the radiant light of his body, the very core of his Vital Energy. No wonder the body withers away at an early age. The "dryness" of his emotions creates dryness and hypo function everywhere in the body: constipation, dry lips, dyspepsia, emaciation and exhaustion reflect the emotional influence on the physical body.

Of course he is a different lover than anyone we have met before. He is a passive lover who lies on his back, hardly participating in the sexual act. He "receives" and expects everything from his partner. He does not like light in the room and prefers to have intercourse in the dark and at night, rarely in the morning. Sometimes it is under the pretext of shame that he turns off the lights, but in reality it is because he wants to concentrate on the act itself and less on his partner. He wants to satisfy himself first. Just like the "Liver" type, he is not averse to a certain degree of violence. Quite the contrary to the "Liver" type, the "Water" type is the non-movement one. Right after the act, he is indifferent, stays immobile and often falls asleep. His favorite erogenous tactile zones are the neck and the back.

Frank's fatigue was resolved with Arsenicum and Natrum muriaticum. He was still a serious, single-minded person, but proud, walking erect and finding joy in his job as a secretary, where he was highly appreciated. The melancholy and deep sadness was gone and, for the first time in a long time, he could look forward to less frustration and a more hopeful future.

The Man Who Lost His Money and His Health

One afternoon, as a good "Liver" type I was playing an all-out tennis match against an opponent who seemed as determined and driven as I was. The match was a seesaw encounter, with both opponents giving in little to the other. In short, the kind of match on which any competitive spirit thrives. Suddenly, my opponent, a scrambling, thin 45 year-old man, stopped and I could see that something was wrong. It was as if all the spirit had been drawn out of him; he looked pale and in agony. "I have to run to the bathroom," he said. When Emmanuel came back, I hardly recognized him. It was like his whole body had gone through a wringer. He apologized for not being able to continue the game as he felt completely exhausted. Disappointed at losing the joy of such a closely matched game I was determined to find out what was wrong.

You know, Luc, this illness has been with

me for at least five years. In fact, I retired
because of it since I can't hold a job under
these circumstances. I can almost predict
day-by-day what is going to happen. Like
clock work, every third day I get an attack
of severe spasms in my esophagus, followed by vomiting and diarrhea. This lasts
for about twelve hours. The next day I am
weak, of course, and need to recuperate.
Then I have a good day but I can't enjoy it
too much because I am already anticipating
the next attack, which never fails to come.
These cycles happen like clock work. I have
lost at least thirty pounds over these last
years. I have seen plenty of physicians, but
no medications have helped, and frankly,
no diagnosis has been made. I am retired
now, and to some extent have resigned
myself to the fact that this is the life I am
going to be living. But it is not easy.

I could believe him. Not only had this mystery illness
cut his working career short, but the constant threat of a
body that seems to react with repulsion is bound to drain
anyone's Vital Energy. Couple the "loss of liquids" (diarrhea and vomiting) with an appetite that borders on anorexia
and Emmanuel's health problems were very serious. As
usual his diagnoses were numerous: esophagus reflex,
esophagitis, gastritis, hiatal hernia, and of course, the always
present "somatization of a neurosis," the polite term for hysteria and hypochondria. But none of these diagnoses was
supported by any objective measures like X-rays or blood
tests, and frankly, I had a hard time believing that Emmanuel,

who loved life and tennis, was a malingerer and hysterical person. There had to be more to this. Emmanuel filled me in, as he had done already so many times before with other doctors.

> I have always been a man somewhat obsessed with my future welfare. From a young age on, my parents taught me to save money for rainy days. They were very careful people and from them I inherited my love for the stock market. I got my first stock when I was 12 years-old and have been playing the market ever since. But a lot of my dreams crashed with the stock market collapse of 1987. I lost a huge amount of money that day. These attacks started shortly after that.

He seems to be another victim of the stock market crash in '87, but a different kind of victim than we met in the "Heart" type. Remember the case of Paul, who also lost his financial nest egg in the same collapse? For him, it was devastating because it did not allow him to live the glamorous life he dreamed of anymore. His personal reaction was a severe depression, a mental disease rather than a physical one. True to the "Water" type, Emmanuel reacted with a physical disturbance to the same event Paul had experienced. It attacked the upper part of his digestive system and the severe spasms, with the explosive vomiting and diarrhea, were a somatization of the intense anger and outrage he felt towards this "betrayal" from an institution in which his whole family had faith. It also was a reflex to the intense fear of poverty he experienced. We already know that one of the biggest fears of the "Water-Man" is his fear of poverty and anxiety about the future. Therefore this financial loss cut right to the heart and concern of someone like Emmanuel. Intense fear turning easily into irritability and anger are "Liver" signs. As we have seen in the "Wood" type, liver and muscle spasms are intimately connected. Putting all these facts together made it easy for me to understand Emmanuel's torturing disease. Even the periodicity of the attacks is used in homeopathy to determine the right remedy. Repetitive doses of China Arsenicum (the poison Arsenicum is coupled to another remedy) finally relieved Emmanuel of these horrendous spasms. He still plays the stock market, but much more carefully. Within months he regained some of the muscle mass he lost in the past, his appetite came back, and you guessed it, I lost the next tennis match. But we both celebrated!

As you have seen in this case, financial loss can have severe repercussions and create an extreme "Water-Man." For this type, financial security means everything. That's why he works hard every day, spends little and tries to put his money in secure investments which will guarantee him a nice cushion for those gloomy days, which in his opinion are bound to happen. When he is successful, he is modest and discrete. When he fails, he is not surprised; he almost expects it. His vulnerability leads to discouragement, disbelief in his reason for existence and sometimes the loss of desire to live. But once you bring him in balance, you will find a competent and confident straight arrow man who always seems to know his goal in life.

The Man Who Lost His Voice

> I am here with my husband, Doctor, be-
> cause he can't speak for himself. He has not
> spoken a word for five years now. All the
> professionals in this city have seen him and
> don't know what to think of it.

Marie, 5'6" and 180 pounds, a real "Earth" type, hov-
ered over her skinny husband, Fred, 56 years-old. His
stooped posture and withdrawn demeanor made him seem
even smaller as he fixed his sad eyes on me. Their was no
hope in his eyes, only resignation. But Marie, down-to-earth,
had patiently asked her husband to write down what had
happened when he lost his voice.

> Fred wrote down that he was looking out
> of the window one day, minding his own
> business when suddenly, he saw a funeral
> passing his door. As he looked more care-
> fully, he recognized the wife of one of his
> best friends, dressed in black, behind the
> carriage and realized with a shock that his
> friend had died. He hasn't spoken since.

A straight forward case for a homeopathic physician, a
complete mystery for a Western medicine doctor. Chinese
medicine also has a clue: sudden fear or frights are related
to the element Water, but as we have seen in Chapter Two,
Water and Fire (which are related to speech) are in the control cycle (Fig. 2). A sudden fright will break the fine balance between Water and Fire and can lead to aphony (loss
of voice) if the trauma is intensive enough. Such sudden

frights can happen many times. These are all the situations from which "you almost died." For instance, you have an almost fatal heart attack. After physical recuperation from this ordeal, the patient is often left with anxieties and worries. This is the same shock you experience when you almost die in a car crash, you almost drown, you almost die in a house fire, etc. This kind of sudden fright will cause severe consequences in a "Water-Man," as it did in Fred. But even to other prototypes, it could cause a layer of "Water" to form on the top of their constitution. "Never well since a fright," which was really the exact diagnosis of Fred, has several homeopathic remedies at its disposition. Opium (homeopathic of course!) and Aconite are fore runners.

These remedies were able to restore the lines of communication between the central organization of the body and the traumatized part involved. As "Like Cures Like," opium, which is known to induce deep sleep, even coma, brought back Fred's speech. The reader should always keep this in mind after any frightful event in his life, and restore without delay the subtle damage done. If not, severe organic disease can be the consequence.

To summarize the causes of a "Water" layer or constitution:

Causality "Water-Man"

Sudden fright, continuous fear, heartbreak, too much standing, excessive intake of salt, financial loss, worry about health, food poisoning, viral infection, grief.

Homeopathic Remedies and Supplements of the "Water-Man"

It is obvious that one of the "Water-Man's" weaknesses are his bones. Osteoporosis can be expected early on in his life. Therefore the Calcium/Magnesium ratio of the "Earth-Man" is necessary here, too. An excellent homeopathic remedy against osteoporosis is Calc. Phos 6x. It is sufficient to take three pellets a day to have excellent protection. As studies have shown that cigarettes boost women's osteoporosis risk, it is wise to quit smoking. Other bone related diseases are arthritis and osteoarthritis, a plague from which so many people suffer. Many of these victims will recognize themselves as being this type, or at least will realize that they have a "Water" layer leading to bone weakness. In "Water-Children," you often find tonsillitis, scarlatina and juvenile acute rheumatoid arthritis. For arthritis and arthrosis, many excellent homeopathic remedies are available (too many to mention here). A homeopathic physician will treat the patient's arthritis, not suppress it. Again, a good homeopathic physician is your best helper in fighting these conditions.

An especially good supplement for arthritis/arthrosis is *evening primrose oil*. The good news about the healing effects of *evening primrose oil* keeps pouring in from research laboratories around the world. Besides controlling blood pressure, it controls inflammation, stimulates natural steroid production and is therefore very effective in reducing the swelling and pain of arthritics. If you want to ease your arthritis further, eat more fish, like salmon, herring, rainbow trout, tuna, whiting, crab, shrimp and cod. They all contain *Omega-3 oils* which appear to lessen the stiffness and aches caused by arthritis. And in case you are not a fish lover, or the fish in your area is too contaminated to eat, you can find fish oil capsules in your local health food store. Take three capsules daily. Other good adjuvants in the fight against arthritis are Bromelain (pineapple enzyme, take three capsules *between meals*) and the antioxidants discussed before: Vitamins A, C, and E. Take them in the indicated doses, usually one capsule daily of each. Add to this Selenium 100 mcg and Zinc 50 mg and you will be a winner. Some herbs, classified as "blood purifiers" help promote urination and can be useful in the treatment of arthritis. These are chaparral, red clover, burdock, echinacea, dandelion and sarsaparilla. Herbs helpful in reducing inflammation are alfalfa, yucca, devil's claw and spikenard.

For impotence and frigidity, many homeopathic remedies are available tailored to each individual's case. But there are some aphrodisiacs in the vitamin world, too. Vitamin E is called the "sex vitamin", Vitamin A is needed for healthy testicular tissue and the production of all sex hormones. To increase testosterone, take a good Vitamin B complex daily. Make sure this complex includes pantothenic acid or B5 since it runs the adrenal cortex. And Vitamin C has emerged as a fertility vitamin since it prevents sperm agglutination (sticking together). It is even claimed that Vitamin C stimulates more intense orgasms. Again, make sure to take the Vitamin C of TAD Corporation with its microdialysis effect.

For protection against prostate disease many homeopathic remedies are available dependent on specific symptoms. Some of the better known homeopathic remedies are conium, clematis, thuja, zinc, selenium, pulsatilla, digitalis, chimophilla and sabal serrulata. Your homeopathic physician will select the right one for you; it is not your task! But no matter which remedy you take, you can add to this a superior product: PG-Plus, from TAD Corporation. It is a natural solution for an enlarged prostate and combines many of the finest products known to influence the prostate. Alanine, glycine, Zinc, Uva Ursi, Bovine prostate concentration and Saw Palmetto Berries are all part of this excellent formula. Take two to four capsules a day.

For recurrent urinary infections, cranberries have been shown to have a tonifying action for the bladder mucosa. Take the capsules (2-3 a day) or the juice. To help in the fight against diabetes, don't forget GTF Chromium, to be taken before meals as outlined under the "Earth" type.

Giving these supplements and homeopathic remedies to the "Water-Man" will be the difference between a miserable, indecisive pessimist and a dependent, sophisticated aristocrat. Ladies and gentlemen, the choice is yours!

EIGHT

Violence and Criminality in Men

Statistics

Is anyone *not* at risk for crime in this country? Violence and murder rates are much higher than we would like them to be in a civilized country. Recent brutal deaths of dozens of young people represent a shocking trend: the young are no longer insulated from violent crime, they are its most frequent victims as well as being the usual perpetrators. So many of these killings are unexplained, senseless murders. It used to be that some "strength" was needed for one person to kill another. There had to be some kind of strange "courage" to harm somebody. Now people can kill just by spraying around gunfire; killing can be done long-distance without having to look someone in the eye. Thirteen year-old kids with guns kill adults for money, fun or no motive at all. Without benefit of maturity, all that's left to keep people from killing other people is morality.

A recent report (February 1995) by the Population Reference Bureau finds that black males in their teens and early 20's are statistically at highest risk to become homicide victims. The homicide rate has ranged from 4.1 per 100,000 people in 1964 to 10.7 in 1980 and continues to rise. It is also interesting to note that the peaks of homicide rates occurred after the stock market crash of 1930, and when the United States pulled out of Vietnam in 1980. Since then, the rate has stayed high. There is no doubt that poverty linked to economical crises, lack of education, increased drug use, dysfunctional families and in general, despair about the future have driven up the crime figures. Families living in small towns can no longer feel safe. I feel that besides addressing the above issues homeopathy, if applied from a young age on, has much to offer to ward off violence and criminality in men. Not only can it soften the blow of grief, indignation, abandonment, loneliness, burn-out, and many more triggering factors, but through application of the constitutional remedy it can strengthen the individual who is more willing and capable of taking care of himself and his family, rather than blaming everyone else. As we have seen in many examples, homeopathy is able to restore the imbalance in the individual before too much damage, emotionally and physically is done. More than any other medical modality, homeopathy can counteract the effects of dysfunctional, criminal hereditary miasms or traits. Some modern examples in this book show this.

The Five Prototypes and Violence

When *unbalanced* each different prototype is capable of violence. As I have described in this book the different emotional and physical characteristics, it is only logical that each type will be violent under different circumstances. Let's look at them one by one.

The "Liver-Wood" Man

The "Liver-Wood" man is probably the most prone to violence. He is the volcano who unexpectedly erupts. He is easily angered, irritated and frustrated, all of which leads to acts of violence when he is contradicted. There are many factors leading to the build-up of possible violence in the "Wood-Man." First of all there is his life-style. Remember, he is the always scheming individual, ambitious and sometimes ruthless in order to get what he wants. When unbalanced, he will do anything that is needed to reach his goal, regardless of the emotion and pain he creates in his environment. He can neglect his family just to bask in the light of adulation and puts a beautiful, young wife on the same level as any of his prized horses, cars, or clothes. This neglect of family and absence of true love and compassion, often leads to violence when the unbalanced "Wood-Man" is confronted by his spouse or family. He is easily offended and very sensitive to criticism, brushing it aside as a nuisance. Often his words are accompanied by hitting and screaming, used to intimidate the opposition. He is more influenced than any other type by various aspects of his life-style which contribute to his violent temper. He is the man most prone to misuse of alcohol and drugs, prescribed or street drugs. They are an integral part of his life used to maintain his already strong physical and emotional constitution. Because "Wood-Men" are often born leaders and successful businessmen, they have the financial means to acquire these substances. It is known that habitual users of drugs become notorious liars, which can lead to violence when they are caught in their maze of lies. At the same time they are used to basking in the adulation of their work, and expect the same kind of intense admiration at home. When this is not forthcoming, the "Wood-Man" often thinks he needs to convince the other party by ever increasing arguments. This leads to frustration and suppression in the abused party while the "Wood-Man," who loves a good fight, walks away without taking into the consideration the feelings of the emotionally destroyed spouse or friend. Fighting physically or verbally is just a way of communication for him.

Then there is the well-known possessiveness of the "Wood-Man." It is his own collector sense that dominates his thinking and acting. Being visible on the throne or in the limelight is a sign of power, and the love of power is strongest in the "Wood-Man." A wife is part of the "collection." No wonder then that passionate crimes are high on the list of "Wood-Men." Even when there is no love between the two parties, he will not let go of the spouse without stalking her, abusing her and threatening anyone coming into her life. He is hurt only in his pride, not in his heart like the "Water-Man." How can anyone leave such a successful, beautiful and ebullient person who seems to score high on all the social popularity polls? It is inconceivable that there is anyone else out there who will get preference over him. His wounded pride leads to the passionate murder, which will carry all the traces of his violent character. It will not be premeditated, but on the spur of the moment. Usually knives, axes, crow bars or any blunt object will do to release the pent-up anger in the act of violence. Often after the act, when the volcano is calm, he will be in a daze and a state of self-denial. The "Wood-Man" can have a split personality: a terror to his loved-ones, a popular, loved individual everywhere else. The split can be so severe that the "Wood-Man," after committing the crime, honestly believes that it is not him who committed this brutal act. And his actions after the crime often confirm this. The denial is so great that he can behave completely normal after committing the most horrible deed. There is no crying, no depression, no despair, only complete rejection. Therefore, how a "Wood-Criminal" reacts after he commits his deeds should be no guidance for proof of his innocence. He can smile and be totally calm after committing the most horrendous deed. When confronted, he will claim it was another "person" in him who did it, supplying fodder for the insanity plea to his attorney.

His violence can easily be turned towards himself. The already powerful physical "Wood-Man" increases his strength during an anger outburst. Often the rage leads to physical injury to his own body. He will smack his fists on the table, hit his head against the wall, tear his hair out and kick a heavy table, all with seemingly indifference. When he commits suicide, it is according to his style: violently. He hangs himself or more often, puts a gun in his mouth, splattering his brain all over. Not a pretty sight, but well within the realm of the explosive nature of a man who acts on the spur of the moment. As already mentioned, rarely will a "Wood-Man" premeditate his act. Therefore he will leave more traces of his deed behind than any other type and easily will get caught. Remorse is rare. With his disdain for other people and his high intellect, he often justifies his violent act as something that the other party had coming to them for a long time. I read the history of a young serial killer who got caught only after killing six young ladies. When he confessed, he said that he had the urge to do so because when he had sexual intercourse for the first time, he was laughed at because he suffered from ejaculatio praecox (loss of sperm before penetrating his partner). His "justified" revenge on women took the form of brutal rape-murders. How much different could his life, and that of his victims, have been if he would have received the appropriate homeopathic liver remedy (Lycopodium)! In my book, when there is a passionate murder, look either for a "Wood" or

"Heart-Man." History is full of these types and often serial killers are driven "Wood-Men."

The "Fire-Heart" Man

The "Fire-Heart" man is a different species. He definitely has some traits in common with the "Liver-Man." First of all, there is an intense passion in this person. Disappointment in love affairs is a great stimulus for this type to commit murder. The motive is different. It is not possession, rather an insult to his beauty and vibrancy that leads to the passionate deed. "How could she ever leave me? I offered her nothing but fun, excitement and beauty," he says with a sigh. Leaving him for someone else is the greatest betrayal and insult to the man who is the center of attention at every occasion. Not on the strength of his intelligence or his arguments like the "Liver-Man," but on the power of his presence, his vitality and outrageous behavior. "How dare she!" he exclaims while committing his crime in the heat of passion. Of course, his passion is too volatile for him to premeditate any of his vile acts, and thinking is not one of his strengths anyway.

Even more than with his actual deeds, the "Heart-Man" hurts with his tongue. He is very loquacious and acts like a snake. He will not attack you face to face but from another direction. He is spiteful and sarcastic, with an unending flow of cutting words. He loves to fight with his mouth, an over-hasty speech crushing his opponents. His tongue darts in and out of the mouth, sometimes spitting while talking or collecting bubbles of saliva in the corner of his mouth. You can imagine the fight between a "Heart-Person" and a "Liver-Person:" passionate, very violent, fast-moving and exhausting. But, just as a snake does not easily retreat, the

"Heart-Man" knows the weak points of his opponent and goes straight for the jugular. This is THE type that commits sexual murders. The "Heart-Man" has many carnal thoughts and pent-up desires. When he does not have a normal sexual life, he can either get violent or depressed. Jealousy is a prominent trigger in his crimes. Because of a single-minded devotion to his partner, he fights back when his territory is threatened. Then he will plot revenge using his malicious and vindictive nature; he will be a formidable opponent. The film, "Fatal Attraction" shows the "Heart-Woman" who fights "till death do us part," the ultimate fight for what she perceives as belonging to her. The "Heart-Person" is truly the Jekyll-and-Hyde personality.

His favorite weapon, besides his tongue, is a gun. It is quick and does not take a considerable amount of courage to handle since he does not have to look his victim in the eye. Almost any deed is done in a moment of passion, fast and spontaneously. But mostly there is great remorse in the "Heart-Man," lamenting about the loss of his desired partner and at the same time, weeping about the exciting life he is sure to lose. There is no other type who is more inclined to commit suicide than the "Heart-Man." The will to survive, so strongly implanted by Nature, is overcome by his extreme neuroses or psychotic states. Our lives are nothing but brief states of conscientiousness and the termination of this precious period is more painful to a normal human being than any other pain which the process of living may ordain. But there is even some joy in suffering and the "Heart-Man," with his bombastic style, will make sure that his intense pain and suicide have been noticed. Appreciat-

ing physical beauty, he will prefer to commit a clean suicide: no guns, no slashing of wrists, but most likely using
medications or poisons.

The "Earth-Spleen" Man

The "Earth" type is the one least likely to commit violent crimes. As we have seen in this book, he is used to being teased and mentally tortured by his peers from a young
age on. His ability to withdraw into his own shell prevents
much damage. Of course he is very sensitive and he will
only turn to violence when too much is too much, even for
him. Frequently then, his rage is turned towards younger
victims who trust him and who he can overpower even with
his limited physical abilities. His strength is his stubbornness, his best defensive outlet for his injured heart. He is
much slower in everything he does. Rarely will he kill in a
moment of passion, but only after the torment has taken on
monstrous, overwhelming proportions. He looks the most
like the "normal" kid or adult: quiet, shy and popular with
younger kids and friends. His unexpected violent deeds will
shock people. We see all the possible violence in "Liver"
types and even in the melodramatic "Heart" types, but coming from an "Earth" type, it always is surprising. Besides
the tormenting, teasing and being put down because of his
slowness, his weight and the way he looks, another triggering factor to violence is when he feels that his home and
family is threatened. His home is his castle, his ultimate re-
sort where he can withdraw to its safety and comfort. Take
that away from an "Earth-Man" and he will defend it as
furiously as any mother animal against approaching danger.

But normally, the "Earth-Man" abhors violence. Even suicide is rare and will be done only when he feels despair about losing his family, his home, his job or friends, all ingredients important to his peaceful, uneventful life.

The "Metal-Lung" Man

The "Metal-Man's" violent deeds will come almost as a surprise to the outside world, as was the case with the "Earth" type. Because the "Metal" type is a master in suppressing his feelings, an iron-clad mental control masks the inner fire burning in this man. His life is correct, solid, immutable, upright and proper. He seems to be devoid of emotion but when he suffers, it is silent brooding over a committed injustice. A trigger for violence in this man is whatever upsets his routine life style but especially something that goes against justice. For him there is white and black, no shades in between, often leading to an argument with family members or friends who can't adjust to his dogmatic, according to the book behavior. Above all, he values a sense of duty and has no patience with people who try to weasel out of responsibilities. His sense of correctness evokes his irritability, he knows what is right or wrong and will not deviate from that. This is the main reason that criminological behavior is found among this type the least. Even if his wife cheats on him, he will keep his dignity and integrity in the face of this difficulty. If anything, his demeanor will lead to violence against this man for "standing above" everyone else. This sense of superiority raises the ire of other people who lose control over their feelings.

As little as he is a threat to other people, the "Metal-Man" can be a considerable danger to himself. First of all he is always in denial about the seriousness of his physical complaints and therefore fails to attract the attention of his physician. But more so, his internalization of feelings often masks the deep depression and worry about the future. He is anxious about anything in the future. If things are not going well in his life, he seems to be indifferent. But he is the type who plans a suicide in silence whenever his future seems black. When he thinks about nuclear war, overpopulation, Nostradamus' predictions, or anything gloomy and doomy, he will prepare to check himself out. He does not discuss it with anyone and no one can guess it. The suicide is well planned to be sure of a successful outcome. He will ask his doctor how many sleeping pills does it take (his favorite way of committing suicide) or will be sure to consult the right book (like "Final Exit") to avoid any surprises. The worst outcome is to be saved from death for it will expose him as a man who lost control over his life and feelings, quite the opposite of the picture of the super correct gentleman that he always seemed to be.

The "Water-Kidney" Man

At last, the "Water-Man" can be the most tortured soul in this world. His violent acts are driven by revenge and vindictiveness, usually linked to a broken love affair or marriage. From a young age on, he has the image of one great absolute love. When betrayed, he acts with a degree of vengeance matching the intensity of his previous love. "If I can't have her, nobody can," is his motto. Where the "Heart-Man" can be distracted from committing violence because he has just met this other wonderful woman in his life, the "Water-Man" has no desire for another love in his life. He cries in silence, holds grudges and uses all his talents to get back at the partner, including physical and emotional abuse.

Even if the partners stay together, he will never let her forget the "unforgivable sin" she committed and only feels good when the other party feels bad. Frankly, the physical violence will be easier to tolerate than the mental torture directed at the poor victim. When he commits a crime, he is the one most likely to confess. He is the killer with a conscience, which is sometimes preserved against his will. But confessions for this "Water- Killer" act as a catharsis to relieve his deeply recessed pain. He will tell all to "get it off his chest," a load created by guilt. The "Water-Man" wants to confess because it stills his pain and gives him some peace of mind, something that does not come easily to this tortured soul.

His violent acts against others or against himself are planned in detail. Every crime will be premeditated, even a crime of passion, which distinguishes him from the "Heart-Man." He stews for months over the perfect crime and is probably the only type who sometimes gets away with it. His favorite weapon is poison, an "accidental" overdose of medications or an ingenious thought like injecting air bubbles into the veins of his victim. A loss of business or a great deal of money is sufficient to trigger a suicide. Money is valued because of a fear of poverty. When it is lost, life is not worth living. This pecuniary loss is more of a factor in suicide than a broken heart. In the latter, the "Water-Man" prefers to live and to pursue the wrongdoer with his hate. He lives for a cause, not a noble one, but a cause nevertheless. Or he becomes a crusader and will choose a profession in which he finds an outlet to get back at the "criminal." Being a private investigator or a prosecuting attorney satisfies the wrong that happened in his life, becoming a psychotherapist forms a bond with his client against the same kind of injustice he was exposed to.

The Boy-Killer: a True Story

My great interest in crime stories lies in my ability to detect the human motives behind the crime. My background in homeopathy and acupuncture gives me an advantage over other medical doctors when trying to read the mind of the perpetrator. But nothing saddens and moves me more than when I read about children who kill. Many times they seem to be too young to understand what they did and have been failed by society in general, and family in particular. Kids are not born bad, they are made bad. When children get killed in close-knit communities, residents are devastated. Nothing rips a town apart more than if the killer is a child himself. Now that you have read this book, you should be able to identify both the killer and the victim in the following true sad story.

The victim, Derrick, was only four years-old when he was brutally beaten to death in a wooded lot near his home. The only thing more shocking was the identity of the killer: thirteen year-old Eric, a pudgy, freckle-faced youth who lived nearby. The murder jolted the community, which is still trying to come to grips with violence they never thought could happen in their rural community of less than a thousand people. Derrick was a typical pint-size dynamo with blond hair and blue eyes, friendly, precocious and with more energy than he could spend. Eric, his killer, seemed to be an ordinary teenager who liked video games and played drums in the school band. Developmentally, Eric was considered slow. As a toddler he showed delays in walking and talking. He had violent temper tantrums until he was four, banging his head on the floor. He wet his bed till age eleven. With his carrot-colored hair and pudgy body, Eric stood out from the other children. He was the brunt of constant teasing. Because of learning problems, he was held back in school for two years. Often he complained to his mother that he "felt stupid and he was never going to be anybody." Readers of this book will recognize the "Earth-Boy." The teasing, his delayed walking, talking, difficulties at school, physical characteristics which made him stand out, the lack of self confidence and the inferiority complex, all indicate the sensitive, vulnerable "Earth-Boy." I have no doubt that if Eric would have gotten the homeopathic remedy, Calcarea carbonicum, much of his behavior would have been different. For one, his sense of inadequacy and inferiority would have been erased and a crime might well have been avoided. It does not come as a surprise to me that his victim was a frail and younger looking boy. In my opinion, the murder was Eric's pay back for all the teasing and torturing he received from his peers. The only reason he had the "courage" to attack another child was because Derrick was a smaller child, someone he could physically handle. Parents should be warned about these tell-tale signs of criminal behavior in youths and try to correct them with love, attention, redefining heroes, instilling respect and appropriate homeopathic remedies. There is an epidemic of youth violence going on, a problem that goes beyond class, age and race. Many factors come into play: societal changes in family structure, economics and moral culture are just some of them. A rise in single-parent families, divorce, substance abuse and domestic violence places enormous pressure on children. Society's infatuation with violence carries over to children. With the availability of guns, explosive situations are created every day. I feel for both families. Eric's life will never be the same. How is society going to deal with him?

The O.J. Simpson Trial: Cast of Players

This book is not intended to contribute to the hype already raging through this country. It is not my intention to determine the guilt of any party, this is entirely up to the court and its jury system. In this book, I am more intrigued by the players themselves. Using what has appeared in newspapers, magazines and what has transpired in the courtroom on TV, I tried to see what types of men (and women) are part of this trial. Can you recognize the characters of this trial as you read this book? Let's go on a tour and look behind the scenes.

The Defendant: O.J.

This trial might well be called the trial of the century. It has sex, beauty and murder, a real-life novel, one that keeps the nation on the edge of its seat. Because of America's fascination with celebrities in distress even Watergate with issues far more important to the nation pales in comparison.

Here we have an American icon, a black man who rose from poverty to become a successful celebrity beloved by millions. He was the embodiment of success. No wonder that one of the bigger challenges for the prosecution is to show the darker side of O.J., not the man who receives instant adulation from strangers and bank managers and gets cheered on while being chased by the police with "Run, O.J., run!" Knowing the different prototypes, it seems that O.J. is an outspoken "Liver-Man." He is athletic, loves the lime-light of being a celebrity and easily plays the public with a charming smile. He stands out in the crowd and seems to be completely at ease when the spotlight is turned on him. On the throne he is visible to everyone and always seems to enjoy the recognition that comes with being a celebrity. But the prosecution is not likely to show this light side of O.J. Unfortunately, there is no shortage of "scenes in a bad marriage," as it was dubbed in the journals. O.J. has plenty of the dark shades of the "Liver-Man." Above all there is the violence and short-temper belonging to this type. Sworn statements by witnesses show O.J. throwing Nicole, his ex-wife of whose murder he is accused, against the wall, knocking her down on a sidewalk, shattering her windshield with a baseball bat, locking her up in a closet, pushing her out of a driving car and so on. Sudden outbursts of violence at the most unexpected moments, showed the volcanic eruptions of this man. Heard on the infamous 911 call was O.J. threatening, kicking in doors, while screaming obscenities at Nicole. They are all part of an explosive "Liver-Man" pulled out of balance by what the prosecution has called possessive jealousy. There was not only violence, but also humiliation, something an unbalanced "Liver-Man" is well capable of doing. Calling her a "fat pig" when pregnant, putting his hand on her crotch in public while telling everyone present, "This belongs to me," and having sex with her in the middle of a fight, while hitting her, all prove this point. The collector sense of the "Liver-Man" is well-documented in other behaviors of O.J. He appreciates fancy cars, nice houses and a beautiful wife. When she left him, he stalked her even days before her death. What is "his is his" for a "Liver-Man" and he will hang on to things and people, not because he needs or loves them, but because he likes the power over them and the power of owning them. As already mentioned, a "Liver-Man" easily moves on to other relationships, as is the case in O.J. But "collecting" and possessing have nothing to do with love. As we have seen in a "Liver-Person," such a type is capable of committing a passionate crime on the spur of the moment when provoked by the sight of another man trying to pry away what, in his mind, belongs to him forever. Even if O.J. is found guilty by the court, I am convinced that this crime was not premeditated. I am sure that the accumulation of jealousy and suppressed anger was caused by not getting from Nicole what he always did before—constant admiration and the silk glove treatment. Being convicted of wife battery can drive a "Liver-Man" to the edge. But he has to be given the same benefit of doubt, as any type can commit homicide.

The Victims: Nicole Brown Simpson and Ronald Goldman

If anything, the Simpson case has put the spotlight on domestic abuse. "Why do women put up with it? Why did Nicole put up with it? Why didn't friends and family step in? First of all, it was hard to imagine that a popular persona like O.J. could possibly have done this. It is easy to behave differently around the rest of the family and of course, there is always reluctance to intervene in something as very personal as a relationship.

She fell in love with the football star at age 18. It is not hard to see how a naive waitress could fall for a celebrity. Nicole is more of a "Heart-Woman." Outgoing, loves dancing and going to a party, loves dressing up and definitely felt at home in the limelight as much as O.J. Normally, this marriage had all the ingredients for being a good one. According to the generation cycle, they can both satisfy each other. The "Liver-Man" provides the "Heart-Woman" with a good living and a chance to enjoy life because of her talented and hard-working husband. The "Liver-Man" loves the possession of a beautiful radiant "Heart-Wife," because she is a reflection of his success and, as mentioned before, part of a collection of valuable "things."

But there is a danger in such a relationship. The "Liver-Man" likes to keep control over his possessions, recognizing that he is the driving force behind their successful lifestyle. And the "Heart-Woman" does not always like to feel dominated by too strong of a "Liver-Man." She loves the attention (quite innocent) from other men and friends, something which can stir the ire of the "Liver-Man." But all in all, she was a real person to most people, smiling in short, tight dresses and involved in the life of her children.

Ronald Goldman is the true personification of the "Heart-Man." It is not a coincident that he was an aspiring actor and, both being "Heart-People," it seemed quite natural that Nicole and Ron would be friends. Ron came across as being the good-hearted man, drifting happily along with vague ambitions, living day to day. It was one of his good deeds, returning a pair of glasses, that made him an accidental victim.

The Judge and Attorneys

As we have seen, Judge Lance Ito is the prototype of the "Metal-Man." He is meticulous, hard working, able to shift through mountains of evidence, and all this while keeping a tight, controlled leadership over his court. He has developed a reputation for steadiness and scrupulous fairness. As we have seen in Chapter Two, "the Metal-Person" controls the "Liver-Person," the best possible combination of judge-attorney. The judge needs to be able to control the sometimes grandstanding, posturing "Liver-Attorney" to keep the jury's attention on the facts, not bombastic rhetoric. Judge Ito never betrays his emotions: he truly personifies the "Metal-Man" suppressing his feelings, exhibiting a stone face, which is highly desirable in a passionate murder case like this is. He is studious, witty, does not seem to be hurried to make any decision, and often rules with common sense after "a good nights sleep." Most of the time, he seems to be floating on a serene cloud of levelheadedness.

Most of the flamboyant lawyers involved are "Liver" types, of course. The most outspoken one is Robert Shapiro, who loves to bask in the attention of reporters, smiling and posing, visible to everyone. It is no coincidence that one of his hobbies is amateur boxing, reflecting the inner tension in a "Wood-Man." He is showy, flamboyant, vain and has a courtroom style of wounded outrage. The one closest to him is probably Deputy District Attorney Marcia Clark. She is also the personification of the fiery, workaholic "Liver-Person." She does not back down from any of the high-power attorneys on the "dream team" and can appear as abrasive as the opposition. Her former profession and interest, a dancer, reflects the fire within her which finds an outlet in this physical exercise. Defense attorney Johnnie Cochran Jr. is a milder "Liver-Man." He looks elegant in his expensive suits and is the gentle, courtly part of the defense. But he is very effective, with his calm demeanor, in scoring points for the defense with short jabbing punches. He tosses an arsenal of hints, suggestions and arguments into this already explosive case. Even when the defense gets into trouble, as was the case for withholding evidence and witness names, he never lost his temper. His politeness almost convinces you that this was just an "honest mistake" and not a calculated move, which you could expect from such a brilliant attorney. Defense attorney Gerald Uelmen, who looks older than his age, is the typical "Water-Man." He is the one doing a lot of research work, questioning witnesses with an apparent even, gentle grandfatherly style. But the "Cobra," as he is nicknamed, lulls his opponent to sleep before lashing out and scoring heavily. A very valuable person to have on any side is F. Lee Bailey, the flamboyant lawyer from Boston, the most relaxed of the "Liver" types. Known for his high-profile defenses, he seems relaxed, smooth and makes everyone feel like his best friend.

This trial is a battlefield between some of the best lawyers in the country. I can imagine that the trial on TV could serve as an example for any law student who can see the best at work: it looks like a mini-course in law. Whatever the outcome, this trial has captured the imagination of almost everyone in this country.

Choosing a Jury: For the Prosecution and the Defense

The selection of a jury is a vital step in any trial since it affords the litigants a unique opportunity to pick their own judges. "Jury investigation" intends to improve a lawyer's chances of getting a jury favorable to his or her side, and to aid the lawyer in shaping the case for maximum impact on the jury. With so much at stake, the jury research field is growing, involving all kinds of professions, including psychologists, sociologists, market experts, physicians and even psychics. All their investigations are aimed at knowing as much as possible about the prospective juror: his opinions, his loves and hates, his favorite pastimes, his habits, and his educational background. While some of the work is good, a lot of it is terrible, resulting in clients paying a lot of money for poor services. It used to be that in order to be selected as a juror, you needed to know a lot about the defendant and the case. This slowly has evolved to a juror who knows almost nothing about the case presented, making it very hard for some trials to take place in an unbiased atmosphere. Yet, surveys, mock juries in which prototypes jurors are tested and a consultant's time add up to thousands of dollars. It is certainly not available to the average citizen who does not have the connections or money.

In criminal cases, jury research is mainly used by the defense. It really does increase the odds of having a fair trial since the prosecution has an advantage before the trial starts. Most people believe that the indicted person must be guilty of something. In spite of the judge summoning that "the defendant is not guilty until proven" most jurors think the burden of proof is on the defendant. But how do you increase your chances of selecting a good jury favorable to your case? I believe that knowing the prototypes of the jurors and applying the laws of generation, control and destruction to the defendant and the jurors, will lead to a much better system than what we now have.

Take the example of the O.J. Simpson trial. Jurors with clashing personalities could be selected so that a hung jury will become very likely. There is so much DNA scientific evidence in this case, so much technical evidence inundating the jury with minute details that, if I were to choose the jury for the defendant, I would likely choose people with the least education: "Heart" and "Earth-People." These two types will easily get bored with dry evidence; the "Earth" types especially, being slower to understand, will get lost in following the evidence and tune out by falling asleep. If I were in the prosecutor's shoes, I would select "Water" and "Metal" types, who are willing to put their emotions aside and look at the facts. Not only will they suppress their feelings, they will enjoy delving in the pile of evidence to find the needle in the haystack. Of course, it will not be too difficult to find a "Metal" type in the jury box, since he is the most duty bound of all types. He will not offer weak excuses, like the "Heart" type who looks at this boring trial as interfering with his exciting daily, joyful moments and who will do anything to avoid being part of a jury. The "Earth" type is not too excited about it either. It disturbs his peaceful, uneventful life and takes him away from his beloved home more than he wants. The "Liver" type will be a juror if it is a high profile case: it is his chance to be part of history and he usually relates well to the "Liver" attorneys. But he can spell doom for the defense. The "Liver" juror will be such a strong personality that he easily sways other jurors to his side. A risk that the defense simply can't take.

Obviously, the O.J. trial, with its ingredients of the rich, the famous and the sexy people involved, attracts the "Heart-Juror" who enjoys being present on such case. Unfortunately for the prosecution, this "Heart-Person" will follow the debate with her heart, fascinated by a real-life soap opera. The lawyer who speaks to her heart the most gets her vote, not the lawyer who is dry and technical. Of course, having different attorneys, as is the case of O.J., somehow covers all bases in appealing to each of the jurors. The "Liver-Juror" likes the explosive, hot tempered "Liver-Attorney" with his avalanche of facts. The "Heart-Juror" is thrilled and cries when the "Fire-Attorney" appeals to the goodness and love in his heart. The "Metal-Juror" will probably pay more attention to the judge's rulings. Being methodical and unemotional himself, he relates to the judge whom he sees as the leader of the court, ruling with an iron hand. If I were a flamboyant "Liver-Attorney," I would avoid this "Metal-Juror." He will not be swayed by any grandstanding and passionate arguments, he can even be put off by it. (He is in the control cycle!) His vote might well be going against *the attorney*, rather than the defendant, with the same disastrous consequences nevertheless.

Perhaps the most disturbing element of jury research is what it says about the average person's ability to relate to the law. It tends to recommend that the lawyer match the presentation of his case to the preconceived psychological make-up of the juror, not always to the facts. Of course, we can argue that both parties, the prosecution and defense, can take advantage of the process, this is what "voir dire" is all about—supplementing "science" when instinct is not enough. But I believe that it will be much easier for an attorney to choose a juror "profile" by having him answer the forty questions in this book (see Chapter 2). It is as scientific as one can get. When taken into account the fact that the average person may not be capable of rising above his prejudices and biases in the jury room, it becomes very important to know in advance the constitutional make-up of the jury. I believe it is the best built-in control you can buy!

Addendum

All supplements and vitamins mentioned in this book can be ordered from:

TAD Corporation
560 River Road
Fair Haven, NJ 07704
(908) 842-3322 for information
1-800-326-0256 for orders

ABOUT THE AUTHOR

Luc De Schepper, M.D., Ph.D., Lic.Ac., C.Hom, D.I.Hom. born in 1946, is the only physician State-licensed in the US in Western medicine, acupunture and homeopathy. He has a medical license in Belgium (1971), as well as in the states of California (1984) and Colorado (1985). He obtained an acupuncture license in Holland after completing a 3-year course at the Dutch Doctor's Acupuncture Association (1978). In 1980, he obtained his Ph.D. in acupuncture in Paris, France. He studied with masters such as Nogier, Borsarello, Mussat, Lebarbier and Kespi. After immigrating to the U.S.A. in December 1981, he received his license to practice acupuncture in California after passing the state examination in 1982. In 1992, he was awarded the Diploma of the British Institute of Homeopathy (D.I. Hom.) as well as the Certificate in Homeopathy (C. Hom.) of the Hahnemann Academy of North America (Robin Murphy), both 2 year programs in classical homeopathy. He was the award winner, Silver cup, 2nd place of 3,800 entering papers of "The Best Papers on the World Traditional Medicine," in Las Vegas, April 1994. He is fluent in four languages, speaking English, French, Dutch, and German. He is the author of ten books and draws of his experience of having treated more than 300,000 patients in his rich career to teach the lay person about medicine as well as health and well being, while his professional books are used by the student as well as by the licensed professional.

Order Form

Please send (   ) copy(ies) of the book

CANDIDA

The Symptoms, the Causes, the Cure

Unit Price: $10.00
Postage: $3.00
New Mexico Residents add 6.25% sales tax

Ship to:

Name: _____

Street: _____

City: _____ State: _____ Zip: _____

Total purchase amount: $ _____

Method of payment (circle one):   Check   Money Order

PUBLISHNG

Please mail payment to:

Full of Life Publishing
500 N. Guadalupe St., G441
Santa Fe, NM 87501